A GOLDEN REGIONAL GUIDE

WASHINGTON

by
Robert E. Smallman

Edited by
Adolph Suchsdorf, III
and
Herbert S. Zim

A
COMPREHENSIVE
NEW GUIDE
FOR VISITORS
TO THE
NATION'S CAPITAL

GOLDEN PRESS · NEW YORK

CONTENTS

The editors wish especially to thank Mr. Edmund J. Fitzgerald, of the U.S. Department of the Interior, for suggestions on the final manuscript.

Maps by Visvaldis Smith, Roger DePui, and Vincent Kotschar, of Map Projects, Inc.

Library of Congress Catalog Card No. 64-11593.

PHOTO CREDITS:

All photographs by Robert E. Smallman, except the following:

Architect of the Capitol: Page 154. Bureau of Engraving & Printing: 50. Louis Checkman: 67. Corcoran Gallery of Art: 98. Federal Bureau of Investigation: 51. Harper's Weekly: 19 (bottom). Library of Congress: 19 (all except bottom), 22, 34, 63 (right). National Archives: 14, 70. National Gallery of Art: 88-89, 90, 92-93, 96-97. National Park Service, U.S. Department of the Interior: 36-37, 63 (left), 114, 115 (right), 118-119, 123 (top), 124, 126, 127, 128, 129, 156-157. Smithsonian Institution: 75, 77 (right), 81. United Press International: 21, 35, 43. U.S. Army: 84. U.S. Navy: 150.

WASHINGTON, D.C.

The capital city of the United States occupies about 70 square miles on the Maryland side of the Potomac River—a site chosen in 1790 by George Washington himself. This mid-Atlantic location gives the city a climate that is brisk in winter, hot and humid in summer, and magnificent in spring and fall.

The city has the same boundaries as the District of Columbia, an independent area belonging to no state and governed by Congress through a three-man board of commissioners. The city (or District) has a population of 870,000 (1960 census), ninth largest in the nation. The metropolitan area—roughly that enclosed by the new Capital Beltway—has 1,284,000 more. Visitors now total about 8,000,000 annually.

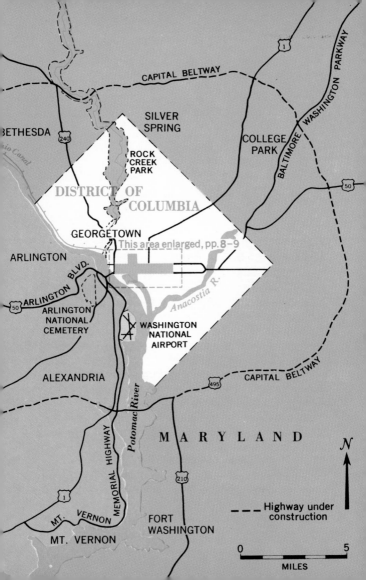

At far left is row of Federal departments, including F.B.I., Archives.

WASHINGTON is a city whose principal business is government, whose principal product is history. Nowhere else in the U.S. is it so easy to feel the past living in the present, to see new history made each day. Examples of this continuity are the Capitol and the White House—buildings almost as old as the nation yet still vigorously involved in the enactment of our future.

The city bears the marks of three centuries. Its basic plan is 18th century—formal, logical, splendid. Realization of the plan is 19th century—utilitarian, ornate, Greco-Roman in feeling, Victorian in taste. Today the feeling is conglomerate. Aluminum, glass, and fluorescence rise over the grandeur of an earlier time.

The capital is a cosmopolitan city. All states have their representatives here, and most foreign countries. Its permanent residents are those who make the city go and some 500,000 career professionals in government. Its transients are mostly tourists—Americans who come, with enthusiasm and respect, to see the nation's political hub.

Principal buildings on Mall are part of Smithsonian complex.

WHERE TO BEGIN: The top of the Washington Monument (pp. 56–59) is the best place for a newcomer to study the layout of the city. Directions can be established and landmarks located while enjoying a magnificent and unobstructed view. Here, too, it can be seen that the city's major attractions—White House, Capitol, Lincoln and Jefferson Memorials—form a cross, centering on the monument. The picture above is a visitor's-eye view, looking due east down the Mall, toward the Capitol.

The details of this area, including the government agencies, museums, and private institutions bordering it, are mapped on pages 8 and 9. The sequence of pages beginning with the Capitol (p. 16) follows a convenient route through the area.

A second map (p. 102) and the page sequence following will guide the visitor through Georgetown and the parks and facilities of Washington "out-of-doors."

A third (p. 143) indicates points of interest within a few hours' drive of Washington.

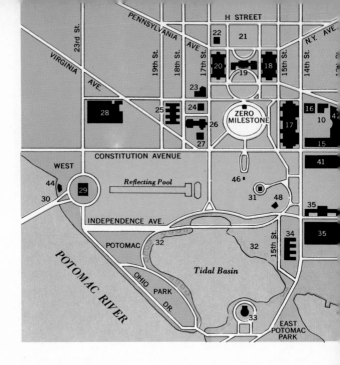

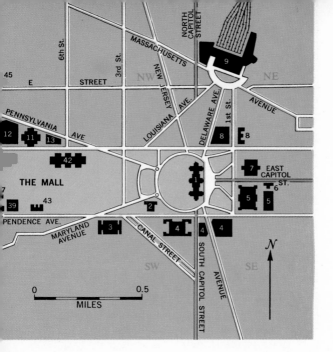

Official gateway to the U.S. for diplomats and other visitors from abroad is John Foster Dulles International Airport. Owned and operated by the Federal government, the huge airfield (covering 9,800 acres) uses the most advanced electronic facilities for all-weather operation. Architect Eero Saarinen's unusual terminal design features a four-acre roof whose 4,000,000-pound weight is suspended on cables slung between 32 concrete pylons.

GETTING AROUND THE CITY

Careful planning will help get the most out of your visit to Washington. Consider your priorities of interest, the distances between points, and the time required to see each place properly. A little quiet map study will determine your best route and cut down on the day's walking. Visiting hours vary; check times listed on pages devoted to places you wish to see. Look ahead to lunchtime so that finding a restaurant doesn't take you out of your way. The National Gallery and Supreme Court buildings have excellent cafeterias, and the Capitol has several good restaurants open to the public. All will be crowded at noontime, so go early or late.

If you have your own car, try to leave it in a centrally located garage or parking lot. Parking space near the major points of interest is extremely hard to find. When driving, watch for one-way streets set at odd angles.

Modern buses give excellent service, both downtown and to outlying areas; check routes at your hotel or motel. (Bus #30, the "tourist special," runs up Pennsylvania Avenue from the Capitol to the White House, on through Georgetown to Washington Cathedral.)

Taxis are one of the city's big bargains. They use a zone system, and most major attractions are in the same zone. Fare: 50 cents for a single passenger, 35 cents apiece for two or more. Try to avoid travel between 7 and 9:30 a.m. and between 4 and 6:30 p.m.

At night, however, the streets are nearly empty. This is a good time to visit the National Archives (p. 70), Library of Congress (p. 26), Lincoln and Jefferson Memorials (p. 60, 64), and the Washington Monument (p. 56)—all open or lighted in the evening. For specific hours check page references above.

L'ENFANT'S PLAN

The capital's unique street pattern should be studied before you set out to see the sights. Most remarkable is the fact that it still reflects faithfully the original plan drawn in 1791 by Pierre Charles L'Enfant, a talented young French architect and engineer who served as a major with Lafayette during the American Revolution. His only instructions from Congress had been to provide a meeting place for the legislature and a home for the President. But L'Enfant had a larger vision and planned so wisely and so well that today the capital city has space, grace, and dignity.

He based his city on broad avenues, the first one (Pennsylvania) connecting two rises about a mile and a half apart, on which he placed the congressional meeting place (the Capitol) and the presidential home (the White House). From these sites other avenues radiated, forming graceful circles where they intersected.

A crisscross grid of streets overlay the avenues. Taking the Capitol as center, the city was then divided into four quadrants—northwest, northeast, southwest, southeast—so that each street address is repeated four times. Each address, however, tells exactly where a place can be found: 1620 D St., N.W., for example, is northwest of the Capitol. D St. is four blocks north, and 1620 is 16 blocks west.

Various embellishments—approaches to important sites, curlicues and shortcuts, new highways—have been superimposed on the original plan. The aerial view of the city gained from the Washington Monument reveals how the radial avenues cut across the gridiron pattern of streets.

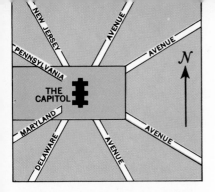

Wide, tree-lined avenues radiating from central points give the city a feeling of leisure, space, and dignity, are named after states. Where they cross, L'Enfant planned grassy, open squares. (He thought these would be ideal artillery sites in case of uprisings or attacks.)

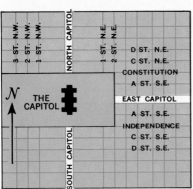

North-south streets generally are designated by numbers, east-west by letters (no B, J, Y, Z). At end of alphabet, streets get two-syllable names in alphabetical order, then three-syllable (A, Adams, Allison), thus giving instant reference to street's distance from Capitol.

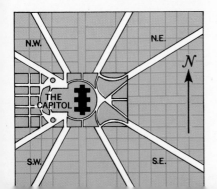

Overlay of avenues, streets, and later additions makes up map of modern Washington. Addresses not followed by quadrant designation are assumed to be N.W., the largest section. L'Enfant plan is not totally consistent, but departures are remarkably few.

13

GROWTH OF A CITY

Philadelphia was the capital of the U.S. in 1790 when, as the result of a political compromise, Congress chose an area ten miles square along the Potomac as the site for a "Federal City." Both North and South had wanted the capital, but the issue was not settled until the Hamiltonians in Congress voted for a southern site in return for the Jeffersonians' support of a money measure.

The site of the District of Columbia was chosen by George Washington, who knew the area well. Land had already been ceded by Maryland and Virginia, and L'Enfant's design, which pleased the first President greatly, was quickly accepted. (Virginia's land was returned to her in 1846.) L'Enfant's plan was laid out by Major Andrew Ellicott, an expert surveyor.

Construction was begun on the "President's Palace," as it was called, in 1792 (Washington did not live to see it completed), and on the Capitol in 1793.

Lincoln's Washington: A view of the capital in 1860.

On December 1, 1800, when the sixth Congress moved to the new capital, Washington was a rude frontier town of about 400 houses and 3,000 inhabitants. L'Enfant's stately avenues were no more than surveyor's markers through meadow and woodland. Only one wing of the Capitol had been finished, only a beginning made on the executive mansion.

In the 19th century the city grew haphazardly. The Washington Monument and the Smithsonian Institution were given fortunate and appropriate locations on the Mall, but much else was done poorly or not at all. Even in Lincoln's day, Pennsylvania Ave. was a dirt road and the railroad was permitted to have its terminal on the Mall. Foreign delegates considered the city barbaric.

Alexander Shepherd, a strong personality, was made head of public works in 1871. He paved and lit the streets, covered sewage-laden creeks, and set aside land for parks. "Boss" Shepherd's domineering tactics got him fired within three years, but in that short period he remade the city. (His statue is on Pennsylvania Ave., near 14th St., N.W.) In 1900, a new parks commission, headed by Sen. James McMillan of Michigan, made L'Enfant's long-abused dream a reality. The Mall was cleared, government buildings were planned, trees were planted, the park system was enlarged.

Another spurt came in the 1930's, when many of the city's current landmarks, such as the Supreme Court, were built. Biggest recent change in the city's profile has come from housing developments on the outskirts to keep pace with the rapid population increase, and from the great redevelopment project under way in the run-down, slum-ridden southwest quadrant.

THE CAPITOL

Stately, serene, and heavy with history, the Capitol is Washington's most familiar symbol of government. It sits on high ground (88 feet above the Potomac), a huge but justly proportioned building whose symmetrical wings flank a majestic cast-iron dome. Capitol statistics are impressive: It is 751 feet long, 350 wide, and 287 high at the tip of Thomas Crawford's statue of Freedom surmounting the dome. (See the original, full-sized plaster model of Freedom at the Smithsonian.) The structure covers 3½ acres, has 432 rooms.

Begin your first visit with the official guided tour. It takes 40 minutes, covers all principal areas faster than you can find them unaided, costs only 25 cents. Enter by the main stairway on the east side (away from the Mall).

Open: 9 a.m. to 3:55 p.m. daily, except Thanksgiving, Christmas, New Year's.

The Capitol was designed by Dr. William Thornton, a versatile physician who was also a poet, portrait painter, and inventor, but who never studied architecture. He was born in the West Indies, emigrated to the U.S. in 1787, and became a citizen the following year. His plan was chosen over 15 others by President Washington, who said it had "grandeur, simplicity and convenience." Thornton died before the building was completed, but succeeding architects, among them Benjamin Latrobe, were faithful to his basic design.

The north, or Senate, wing was completed first and for seven years accommodated 32 senators, 105 representatives, and the three-man Supreme Court. In 1807 the House wing was finished. The British burned the building during the War of 1812; rebuilding, redesign, and expansion went on for years. The great cast-iron dome was not finished until the Civil War. Since then, only one major change has been made: the east front was moved forward 32 feet in 1961 to give the Capitol better architectural balance. The new front is a faithful reproduction of the old façade, which is now an interior wall. It provides some 75 new offices.

All parts of the Capitol are open to the public except private offices and committee rooms during closed sessions. (Open sessions are listed in the morning newspaper.) To enter the visitors' gallery of either House or Senate, obtain a pass at your congressman's office, or join one of the official tours.

Photographs are permitted in Statuary Hall and the Rotunda (a pass from the Capitol Architect's office in the basement is required for a tripod), but not in the rest of the building. Cameras must be checked before you enter either visitors' gallery.

Original Senate wing (above, left) was first part of Capitol ready for use. After House wing was completed in 1807, the two sections were joined by a wooden walkway (above, right). In this sketch of the 1820's the basic Thornton plan is shown as conceived by an artist (right). Below: Actual erection of epic 4,500-ton dome was a major engineering feat in 1860's. Large dome was needed to balance new House and Senate extensions.

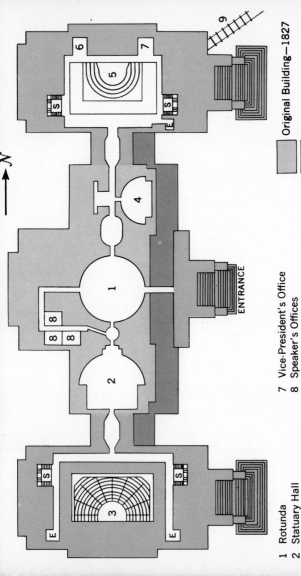

N →

Original Building—1827
Wings Added—1857
Front Extension—1961

ENTRANCE

1 Rotunda
2 Statuary Hall
3 House of Representatives
4 Old Senate Chamber
5 Senate
6 President's Room

7 Vice-President's Office
8 Speaker's Offices
9 Senate Subway
S Stairways
E Elevators up to Visitors' Galleries,
  down to House and Senate Restaurants

THE HOUSE OF REPRESENTATIVES sits in the world's largest legislative chamber—93 by 139 feet—in the south wing. The presiding officer is the Speaker, whose authority is symbolized by the mace resting on a marble block on the rostrum. It consists of a silver ball and eagle surmounting 13 ebony rods, and has been used on occasion to restrain overwrought congressmen engaged in fisticuffs.

House seating is arranged so that Republicans are on the Speaker's left, Democrats on his right. Seats are chosen by congressmen in order of seniority. Preferred places are in the front rows or along the aisles.

The large portraits of Washington and Lafayette flanking the rostrum have hung in the House since 1832. Around the chamber are medallions of 23 historic figures who have contributed to the evolution of the law. They include Moses, Justinian, Napoleon, Blackstone, and Thomas Jefferson. The present walnut paneling and gray marble of the House were installed during the latest redecoration of the chamber in 1951.

Press gallery is above Speaker's rostrum in House of Representatives.

Early House of Representatives chamber, now Statuary Hall,
witnessed debates by Henry Clay, Daniel Webster, John Calhoun.

THE SENATE meets in the Capitol's north wing. Its chamber, reconstructed in 1950 to provide modern improvements, still contains 45 senatorial desks dating from 1839. Each has the names of its occupants under the lid. Tradition dies hard in the Senate. On either side of the rostrum stands a tiny enameled snuffbox. Although unused, the boxes are faithfully refilled once a week. In niches spaced around the walls are busts of the first 20 Vice-Presidents, all of whom presided over the Senate. Entrance to the public galleries is on the gallery floor, accessible by elevator or handsome marble stairways at either end of the wing.

Visit your local representatives at their nearby office buildings (north and south of the Capitol). Congressmen usually have more time for their constituents than senators, but the office staff of either will welcome you and help with touring suggestions, literature, or setting up appointments at government agencies.

STATUARY HALL, south of the central Rotunda, was the original House of Representatives. Here for more than 50 years affairs of state were debated. A bronze floor plaque marks the spot where John Quincy Adams, the only President to return to Congress after serving his term, died at 81. From this same spot, thanks to remarkable acoustics, a whisper can be heard across the hall. Today statues of marble and bronze ring the chamber. They memorialize distinguished sons and daughters from each state.

The old Senate Chamber, in the first section of the Capitol to be completed, is on the north side of the Rotunda. Vice-President Thomas Jefferson presided at its first meeting in 1800. Here the Louisiana Purchase and Missouri Compromise were debated and ratified and 18 states admitted to the Union. In 1859, when the Senate left for its present quarters, the Supreme Court moved in, used the room for 75 years.

Huge painting of Admiral Perry at the Battle of Lake Erie (1813) hangs in Senate stairway. Constantino Brumidi's meticulous and colorful murals decorate the Capitol dome, Senate hallways (right), and the Rotunda frieze. Many panels include native American birds and animals.

CAPITOL CORRIDORS are fascinating to wander. Most of them display historical paintings, prints, and sculpture. In the Senate wing, the walls also are elaborately decorated. The House wing is more austere because congressmen of the 1850's objected to the employment of foreign artists to decorate the Capitol.

Restaurants open to the public are situated on the street-level floor of both wings. Try the traditional bean soup, always on the menu. At basement level, the main hallway runs the length of the building (751 feet), past 40 sandstone pillars supporting the dome.

24

The Capitol has most of the services and facilities of a decorous gentleman's club. On the main floor are barber shops, a bank, a post office, a railroad and airline ticket office. There are offices for the Capitol Physician, the Senate Chaplain, and the Chief of Capitol Police.

It has a recording studio, a campaign photo room, and, on the gallery floor, a clock-repair shop. In the basement are the offices of the Capitol Architect, responsible not only for this building and its grounds but for others, including House and Senate offices, Supreme Court, and Library of Congress.

LIBRARY OF CONGRESS 1st & INDEPENDENCE, S.E.

An imposing—and increasing—total of more than 41,283,000 items, including books, manuscripts, maps, sheet music, historic prints, photographs, phonograph records, and motion-picture films, make the Library of Congress one of the world's great accumulations of human knowledge.

Started for the exclusive benefit of Congress in preparing legislation, it is now a reference library for public use. A staff of 2,700 persons gives rapid and courteous service at no charge.

Congress established a library of 3,000 books in the new Capitol in 1800, but these were used for tinder when the British burned the building during the War of 1812. Afterward, Thomas Jefferson sold Congress his personal library (some 6,500 volumes), probably the finest in the country at that time, for about $24,000. From this nucleus has grown the present collection, stacked on 270 miles of bookshelves. The law library alone numbers well over 1,000,000 volumes, the science collection half again that many. L'Enfant's original plan of Washington is among 2,500,000 maps. Most of Mathew Brady's Civil War pictures are among 3,000,000 photographic negatives, prints, and slides.

On the main floor, you can see Jefferson's first draft of the Declaration of Independence, the Gettysburg Address in Lincoln's handwriting, and a Gutenberg Bible printed in 1455.

The original library building, completed in 1897, is augmented by a five-story annex across 2nd St.
Open: 9 a.m. to 10 p.m., Mon. through Fri.; noon to 6 p.m., Sat.; 2 to 6 p.m., Sun. and holidays, except Christmas and July 4.

Neptune fountain (above)
stands at Library entrance (top).
Exterior is in Italian
Renaissance style. Library's
huge proportions can be
seen in floor-to-ceiling view of
main reading room (left).

27

SUPREME COURT

1st & EAST CAPITOL, N.E.

The Supreme Court building is one of the most beautiful in Washington. Designed by architect Cass Gilbert and completed in 1935 at a cost of $3,000,000, the Court is in the style of a classic Grecian temple, with Corinthian columns of white Vermont marble which turn golden in the afternoon sun. On the frieze above the columns is inscribed "Equal Justice Under Law."

The building was the first home the Court could call its own. Since 1801, the justices had met in various rooms of the Capitol and were always cramped for space. Now they have a special auto entrance that leaves them at a private elevator to their quarters. Each justice has a suite of three rooms, and may use a main dining room and a library of 75,000 volumes.

The justices preside in an impressive, dimly lit, high-ceilinged courtroom. They sit in old-fashioned, high-backed leather chairs, four on either side of the Chief Justice, in descending order of seniority. Behind them are four Doric columns of Italian marble and drapes of rich red velvet.

The Court meets every other fortnight from October to June. It sits from noon to 4:30 p.m., Monday through Thursday, and its sessions are open to the public. The courtroom (capacity: 144 seats) often is crowded on Mondays when decisions are handed down. When the Court is not in session, there are conducted tours of the building every 15 minutes. An excellent cafeteria is open to the public for breakfast and lunch.

Open: 9 a.m. to 4:30 p.m., weekdays; 9 a.m. to noon, Sat.

The highest judicial power in the U.S. rests with the Supreme Court. The Court is concerned only with the meaning of the Constitution—the supreme law of the land—and hears only cases requiring a constitutional interpretation. Through its privilege of "judicial review," it may nullify any Federal, state, or local law which, in its opinion, violates any provision of the Constitution. (Most of the laws the Court has overturned have originated in the states.)

Oddly enough, the Court has no means for enforcing its decrees. Traditionally, however, Americans have respected the Court and acceded to its decisions.

Like any human institution, the Supreme Court has had its great and lesser men, its great and lesser moments. Of the 94 justices who have served it, perhaps the most influential was John Marshall, of Virginia, who became Chief Justice in 1801. For 34 years thereafter, in a series of notable decisions, he established the principle that the interests of the national government shall have priority over those of other agencies and parties. And by sheer force of character, he also established, in practice as in theory, the parity of the judiciary with the legislative and executive branches.

Among the giants of the modern era was Oliver Wendell Holmes, Jr., of Massachusetts, who sat for 29 years, until the age of 91. Known as "the Great Dissenter," Holmes was one of the Court's profound philosophers and lived to see many of yesterday's dissents become tomorrow's precedents.

Supreme Court justices are appointed for life terms (subject to good behavior) and are paid $35,000 a year. (The Chief Justice gets $500 more.)

Portrait of Chief Justice John Marshall (right) hangs in main floor conference room. Above: Cantilevered bronze-and-marble spiral staircase (viewed from top) is one of a pair flanking central Memorial Hall.

THE SUPREME COURT'S JOB

Interpreting the Constitution is a subtle task. There are aspects of American life on which the great document is silent (presidential succession), others on which its guidance is general ("due process"). And it must be applied to social and economic conditions that have developed in ways undreamed of by the Founding Fathers.

Much of what lawyers and scholars believe the Constitution to mean, therefore, is contained in the accumulating decisions of the Court and the precedents they establish. As times change, however, the character of the Court may also change. New justices may be appointed who bring a different legal philosophy to the bench. Or the Court, which is privileged to select the cases it will hear and decide, may find itself involved in new areas of interpretation.

Then, old precedents may be overturned, and in the majestic and reasoned language of the Court, a new statement of the meaning of constitutional freedom will be made for all the people of the United States.

Giant palm trees
hung with climbing vines
(left) tower above
trickling jungle stream in
Botanic Gardens. In a
section simulating
a tropical rain forest,
orchids (below) grow
in profusion. The gardens
attract thousands of visitors
during the Easter season
when early spring
plants (below, left) appear.
Capitol grounds (right)
are landscaped with
a great variety of trees
and flowering shrubs.

THE CAPITOL GROUNDS (above), which form the east end of the Mall and total 131 acres, are a fine setting for the venerable building on the Hill. Since several climate zones overlap in Washington, a variety of trees, plants, and shrubs flourishes on the grounds. Many of these are identified by tags for the stroller.

THE BOTANIC GARDENS replace a rambling old Victorian greenhouse that once stood at the foot of Capitol Hill. The present aluminum-and-glass structure, just below the House wing, has an array of tropical plants from all over the world and has recreated a section of exotic jungle. The Gardens display domestic plants in season. Chrysanthemums begin in November, followed by poinsettias at Christmas, azaleas in spring, and a magnificent Easter show.

Open: 9 a.m. to 4 p.m., Sun. through Fri.; 9 a.m. to noon, Sat.

View of pre-Civil War Mall from Capitol's west portico.

THE MALL

Pierre L'Enfant's ''Grand Avenue'' is much as he planned it in 1791—a mile-long, 400-foot swath of parkway running from the Capitol to the Washington Monument. L'Enfant expected it to be bordered by gardens and did not dream that the many elements of Mr. Smithson's institution would find their home there. But basically it has the spaciousness he wanted.

West and East Potomac Parks (sites of the Lincoln and Jefferson Memorials) did not exist in L'Enfant's time. The riverbank was at what are now Constitution Ave. and 17th St. The continuation of Constitution, past the Ellipse and along the base leg of the Federal Triangle, was a waterway—Tiber Creek. This meandered past the base of Capitol Hill (then Jenkins Hill), and southward to the Anacostia River. Part of its route can be traced along still-existing Canal Street. It was not filled in until late in the 19th century, about the time the railroads moved tracks and terminal from the Mall to the present site of Union Station.

Breadth of Pennsylvania Ave. makes it ideal for parades.

PENNSYLVANIA AVENUE

The most famous stretch of Washington's most famous street is the mile and a half of Pennsylvania Ave. between the Capitol and the White House. (Total length: 6½ miles, from Rock Creek to the Anacostia River.) This is the parade route for inaugural processions, troop reviews, and welcomes to distinguished visitors.

Pierre L'Enfant planned an uninterrupted view from Capitol to White House, but Andrew Jackson changed that in 1833, when his architects could not agree on a site for the Treasury Building. He arbitrarily located it in the middle of Pennsylvania Ave., making a permanent break in both thoroughfare and view.

THE FEDERAL TRIANGLE: Much-needed office space for the expanding Federal government was developed here in the 1930's. From the apex at the junction of Pennsylvania and Constitution Aves. to the base at 15th St. are: Federal Trade Commission, Archives, Justice Department, Internal Revenue, and Post Office, Labor, and Commerce Departments.

THE WHITE HOUSE

1600 PENNSYLVANIA AVE.

An Executive Mansion showpiece is the Red Room, newly restored as an Empire parlor of the early 1800's. Its walls are hung in cerise silk with gold scroll borders, and the same colors are repeated in upholstery of French and American period furniture. Public tour of White House includes Red, Blue, and Green Rooms, the state dining room, and the gold-and-white East Room. The White House was only recently made a national monument.

White House visiting hours are: Fall and winter from 10 a.m. to noon, Tues. through Sat.; spring and summer from 10 a.m. to noon, Tues. through Fri.; 10 a.m. to 2 p.m. Sat. and holidays. Although the tour takes only 20 minutes, there may be a sizable waiting line in spring and summer. Write your congressman in advance for tickets to special 8:30 a.m. tour.

George Washington picked the site for this conservatively handsome "President's Palace" and approved the design, which won a $500 prize for architect James Hoban. Washington also kept an interested eye on the building's progress (the sandstone walls were quarried near Mt. Vernon), but died before it was completed.

The first occupant of the mansion was John Adams, second President of the U.S., who moved there in 1800. He liked to swim in the Potomac before breakfast, and his wife Abigail dried the presidential laundry in the East Room (where formal receptions are held today).

From that time to this, the White House has reflected the taste, the personality, and the style of its tenants. It has been remodeled or changed during almost every administration and completely rebuilt on three occasions. Only 14 years after it was finished, the British burned it when they invaded Washington during the War of 1812. Dolley Madison, who had planned a dinner party that night, instead packed a trunk with important government papers, cut the famous Stuart portrait of Washington from its frame, and skipped town. Only a shell remained when the British left. After the interior was rebuilt, the smoke-blackened sandstone was painted white and people began calling the place the "White House."

Historic first-floor state rooms are part of public tour.

Extensive rebuilding was not undertaken again until 1948, when a leg of Margaret Truman's piano sank through the floor. Examination proved the whole structure to be deteriorated and dangerously unsound. It would have been cheaper to demolish it and start over again, but 150 years of history could not easily be cast aside. The Trumans moved into Blair House, across the street, and the White House was stripped down to its original sandstone walls.

A steel framework was erected for support. New heating, air conditioning, and electrical systems were installed. And all old panels, moldings, doorframes, and appointments were carefully preserved and returned to their original location. By 1952, at a cost of some $5,400,000, the job was finished.

In 1961, Mrs. Jacqueline Kennedy began redecorating the White House public rooms with period furniture and art bearing on U.S. history.

The White House is situated on 18 acres of beautifully landscaped grounds which are planted with nearly 400 trees. Some of them date from 1826. In its time, the huge south lawn has served to graze presidential cows and sheep, been used as a putting green and touch-football field, and for Easter-egg rolling and helicopter take-offs.

State dining room seats up to 120 guests beneath Healy portrait of Lincoln.

Huge Christmas tree (left) on Ellipse, south of the White House, traditionally is lighted by the President. Its illumination begins the annual Pageant of Peace, week-long music and dance program. Main entrance to the White House (right) is reserved for official visitors. Tours begin at gate on East Executive Ave.

Thomas Jefferson thought the White House spacious enough to accommodate "two Emperors, one Pope, and a Grand Lama." But this was at a time when the executive branch of the government was small and a President could conduct his business in one room on the second floor in an atmosphere of democratic informality. Throughout most of the 19th century anyone wishing to see the President simply walked into the White House and presented his card. And several times a year public receptions were held in the East Room at which the President greeted and shook the hands of literally thousands of visitors.

By Theodore Roosevelt's time, however, the residential areas of the White House were being overwhelmed by the presidential. To provide new office space and restore a measure of privacy to his family, T. R. had the east and west wings built. The east wing is the main public entrance to the White House. The west wing contains the President's office and Cabinet Room, space for key staff members, the press information room, and radio and TV broadcasting equipment.

Today the public and private life of the White House still are unavoidably mingled, but sensibly controlled to assure the efficiency, convenience, and safety of the President. (Security provisions of the Secret Service and the Executive Mansion guards are numerous but inconspicuous.) The public tour is confined to the historic state rooms of the ground floors. Upper floors are reserved to the President's family and guests. Here are the famous Lincoln Room, containing his bed and a copy of the Gettysburg Address; the Oval Room, formerly a presidential study but now a drawing room; and the President's dining room.

All told, the White House and its wings contain 132 rooms, 20 baths, five elevators, and a swimming pool. Two basement floors extending beneath the lawn provide space for the kitchen, heating plant, and bomb shelter.

Dimensions: The main building is 170 feet by 85, has six floors. The east and west wings are three stories high. The mansion and its grounds require a house-keeping and maintenance force of some 70 persons.

Presidential helicopter taking off from south lawn of White House symbolizes wider range of Executive Department today.

THE PRESIDENCY

The President of the United States has the world's most complex job. He is responsible for the largest branch of the world's largest government: ten cabinet departments, 2,000 executive agencies, 2,000,000 Federal employees (excluding the military). He is commander in chief of the armed forces. Through the legislative program he recommends to Congress, he is the nation's chief domestic planner and often its chief architect of foreign policy. And he is automatically his party's chief politician.

Article II of the U.S. Constitution also confers on him the power to make treaties (with the consent of two thirds of the Senate), nominate Federal judges, ambassadors, ministers, and consuls (subject to senatorial confirmation), receive foreign diplomats, commission officers in the armed services, and grant pardons for all Federal offenses, except impeachment.

The President's powers have increased greatly in this century—and so, too, have his responsibilities. In a growing and ever more complicated nation, people have looked to the Federal government for assistance in combating their economic and social problems. And thus have arisen the executive agencies whose effect is felt today at every level of American life. (Congress, the dominant governmental power of the 19th century, has lost some of its initiative and influence, although it still can veto a President's program.)

The nation's assumption of a leading role in world affairs has intensified executive responsibilities in such fields as foreign aid, global monetary problems, and the U.N., whose U.S. representative is of cabinet rank.

Salary: The President receives $100,000 a year (subject to income taxes), plus a $50,000 taxable allowance to help defray expenses resulting from the performance of official duties; also available: a $40,000 nontaxable allowance for travel and official entertaining.

Honor guard greets visitor on White House lawn.

EXECUTIVE DEPARTMENTS

Most of the executive agencies are the responsibility of the ten cabinet departments. Many of them have at least one interesting operation the public may visit. The following, unless otherwise noted, are **open 9 a.m. to 5 p.m., Mon. through Fri.**

SECRETARY OF STATE traditionally is ranking cabinet officer. State Department assists the President in developing foreign policy, administers Foreign Service, maintains liaison with U.N., runs Peace Corps, issues passports, and has many other duties.

Department of State, 23rd & C, N.W., offers a guided tour which includes the first-floor auditorium where presidential press conferences are televised, the impressive International Conference Suite, and the Great Seal of the United States. **Open: 7 a.m. to 6:15 p.m., Mon. through Fri.** (The old State Department building, an architectural curiosity in French neoclassic style, is west of the White House. It now houses several executive agencies, such as the Budget Bureau.)

SECRETARY OF DEFENSE is civilian head of the Army, Navy, and Air Force Departments, which were unified in 1947. Space Agency (NASA) and Central Intelligence (CIA) are not under Defense Department.

The Pentagon, across the Potomac in Arlington (although its address is Washington 25, D.C.), is the world's largest office building with a population of about 27,000. It is five stories high, has five concentric rings of offices on each floor, and 17½ miles of corridors. Military exhibits are on display, but most of the building is restricted. **Open: 7 a.m. to 6 p.m., Mon. through Fri.**

Most visible evidences of the Defense Department in the capital area are the following units:

THE ARMY'S "OLD GUARD" (1st Battle Group, 3rd Infantry) has the longest continuous history of any U.S. army unit. Originally formed of veterans of the Revolution, it came into existence shortly after the Constitution was ratified (1793). Based across the Potomac at Fort Myer, Virginia, it handles ceremonial events in the Washington, D.C., area, including the 24-hour-a-day guard at the Tomb of the Unknowns. The Colonial Fife and Drum Corps of the Old Guard, activated in 1960, is dressed in uniforms of the Revolutionary period and performs at special events of military and historical significance. Check at Arlington Cemetery for its current schedule.

THE MARINE BAND, in Washington since 1801, performs at official ceremonies, greets visiting heads of state. It may be seen at the Marine Memorial (p. 136) on Tuesdays at 7:30 p.m., June through August, or the Friday evening parades at Marine Barracks (p. 133) 9 p.m. at 8th & I Sts., S.E., June 1 through Labor Day.

Old Guard Colonial Fife & Drum Corps performs martial music, close-order drill, and skits of camp life during Revolution. Check Fort Myer for current schedule. Colorful costumes are authentic to the last button; instruments are replicas of antique originals.

ATTORNEY GENERAL enforces Federal laws through Justice Department, represents the government in court cases, gives legal advice to Federal agencies, supervises Federal prisons, Immigration & Naturalization Service, and F.B.I.

Department of Justice, Constitution & 9th, contains the fascinating F.B.I. Museum (p. 51).

SECRETARY OF THE TREASURY collects taxes (Internal Revenue) and duties (Customs), makes currency (Bureau of Engraving, the Mints), guards against counterfeiting (Secret Service), runs Coast Guard, Narcotics Bureau, T-men.

Two rooms in the main Treasury Building, east of the White House, are used as exhibit rooms to which the public may go, but Bureau of Engraving & Printing (p. 50) is only department open to visitors.

SECRETARY OF AGRICULTURE, among many functions, offers marketing and research services, deals with crop insurance, farm surpluses, and subsidies, runs Soil Conservation Service, Rural Electrification Administration, Forest Service, Commodity Credit.

Alexander Hamilton, first Secretary of the Treasury and financial genius who was responsible for monetary policies of infant U.S., stands outside capriciously placed Treasury Building, which blocks view from Capitol to White House.

Department of Agriculture, 12th & Independence, S.W. (on Mall), has temporary exhibits, shows films in the patio. Its most interesting work is done at the Agricultural Research Center at Beltsville, Maryland, 12 miles north of Washington on Rt.˙1. For guided tour of Beltsville phone GR 4-6500.

SECRETARY OF COMMERCE is concerned with business and economic growth, here and abroad; also runs Bureau of Standards, Patent Office, Census and Weather Bureaus, Coast & Geodetic Survey, Civil Aeronautics Administration.

Department of Commerce, 14th & Constitution, N.W., has industrial exhibits in the lobby and a fascinating electronic chart that continually registers all births, deaths, and other statistics. It also has a patent-research room and a museum of patent models. In the basement is a fine aquarium. **Open: 8:30 a.m. to 4:30 p.m., Mon. through Fri.**

POSTMASTER GENERAL has oldest cabinet job, first held by Benjamin Franklin in 1775. Position may have political overtones because of tremendous patronage involved, is often given to the President's campaign manager.

New Post Office Building, 12th & Pennsylvania, N.W., has a philatelic salesroom (Room 1315) where any U.S. stamp still in circulation may be purchased, also displays of rare U.S. and foreign stamps.

SECRETARY OF LABOR is concerned with employment, working conditions, and labor-management relations. Under his supervision are the Bureau of Labor Statistics, Women's Bureau, and wages & hours and employee compensation divisions, 14th St. & Constitution Ave., N.W., (none of which can be visited).

SECRETARY OF THE INTERIOR runs a department concerned with natural resources: Bureau of Mines, Fish and Wildlife Service, National Park Service, Indian Affairs, Land Management, Reclamation Bureau.

Department of Interior, 19th & C, N.W., was the city's first modern office building more than 30 years ago, is still one of its finest. More than 30 large murals decorate the corridors, many of them by leading artists of the 1920's and 1930's. A sizable museum on the main floor displays the department's wide-ranging activities. Across the hall, a small shop offers Indian and Eskimo art and craftwork. **Open: 7:45 a.m. to 4:15 p.m., Mon. through Fri.**

SECRETARY OF HEALTH, EDUCATION & WELFARE has newest cabinet post, created in 1953. Responsibilities include Social Security, Public Health Service, Food and Drug Administration, Children's Bureau.

Department of H. E. & W. building, Independence and 3rd, S.W., has no public exhibits of its own, but does house the Voice of America studios **(open to visitors 11 a.m. to 3 p.m. weekdays),** which broadcast around the clock in 38 languages.

Many interesting and unusual agencies are unfortunately not open to the public. Neither the Central Intelligence Agency nor the Secret Service invites publicity, for obvious reasons. The Food and Drug Administration (in the Agriculture Building's basement) welcomes visitors, but prefers them to phone first. Also busily working in the public's interest, although not open to public scrutiny, are the National Bureau of Standards, the Weather Bureau, the Civil Aeronautics Administration, the National Science Foundation, the Census Bureau.

John Steuart Curry's mural of "Oklahoma Land Rush" (above) adorns north lobby of Interior Department's fifth floor. Small shop on main floor sells Indian and Eskimo crafts, like Hopi Katchina doll (right) and fine Navajo silverwork (below).

BUREAU OF ENGRAVING AND PRINTING 14th & C, S.W.

People's fascination with the sight of money being printed has made the bureau, situated about midway between the Washington Monument and the Jefferson Memorial, one of the capital's most popular tourist attractions.

A 25-minute guided tour takes the visitor along cat-walks overlooking the presses that produce a daily average of over $30,000,000 worth of paper money. Actually, since the entire manufacturing process takes 31 days, there may be as much as $150,000,000 going through the bureau at any moment. Most new money replaces worn-out bills; a $1 bill has an average life of 15 months and its replacement cost is one cent. The Bureau produces bills in every denomination up to $100,000, also prints postage and revenue stamps, bonds, treasury notes, officers' commissions for the military, invitations to White House receptions, and other miscellaneous engraving.

Open: 8 a.m. to 11 a.m., and 12:30 p.m. to 2 p.m., Mon. through Fri.

Fascinating Washington tour is through the Bureau of Engraving & Printing, where visitors may watch employees prepare currency for distribution. Bills are counted at least 12 times during manufacture, either by hand (as at left) or by machine.

Agents practice marksmanship in F.B.I.'s basement range.

F.B.I. 9th & CONSTITUTION, N.W.

The Federal Bureau of Investigation has an exciting, hour-long tour of its headquarters in the Department of Justice building. A young G-man will be your guide.

Displays of weapons and photographs trace the history of the F.B.I. since 1924, when J. Edgar Hoover became its first director. At the Identification Division, where some 160,000,000 fingerprints are on file, technicians show how an incoming print or set can be matched from the file within minutes. A visit also is made to the laboratory, which employs 220 scientists and technicians to conduct more than 160,000 examinations each year of cars, clothing, blood, dust, lint, handwriting, and bullet shells. The tour ends at the basement target range.

As the investigative branch of the Justice Department, the F.B.I. has jurisdiction over all violations of Federal law except those assigned to other agencies (such as the Secret Service's responsibility for counterfeiting). The F.B.I. also investigates all reports of espionage, sabotage, and treason.

Tours: 9:15 a.m. to 4:15 p.m., Mon. through Fri.

Rampant eagle is detail from pointing statue of
Lafayette. Much of city's statuary is flamboyant and elaborate,
as, for instance, the life-sized artillery
battery in action on Grant Memorial. Opposite page:
Memorial to World War II's Second Division.

HEROES: AHORSE AND AFOOT

Washington is a city of statues, most of them creations of the 19th century, which loved to commemorate its famous men and stirring events in metal and stone. The National Capital Region National Park Service is in charge of about 100 outdoor memorials, mostly statues, and there are many others not under its jurisdiction. (The Capitol, excluding its grounds, contains more than 150 statues and busts.)

Elaborate statuary groups are common. On the Mall, just below the Capitol is a massive monument to Ulysses S. Grant whose marble platform is 250 feet long and 70 feet wide. This huge base enables a life-sized cavalry charge to take place on one side while a battery of artillery is in action on the other!

Lafayette Park, directly across Pennsylvania Ave. from the White House, has five major monuments in

its two-block area. On high pedestals, one at each corner of the park, are figures of Revolutionary heroes from abroad—Lafayette, Kosciusko, Rochambeau, and von Steuben. In the center of the park, Andrew Jackson sits astride a rearing charger, calmly tipping his hat—the first memorial executed by famed sculptor Clark Mills.

More unusual memorials include seven aluminum sea gulls in flight (Navy-Marine Memorial, Columbia Island); the mast and conning tower of the battleship Maine, near the Arlington Cemetery amphitheater; a Japanese lantern and pagoda commemorating Commodore Perry's visit to Japan in 1854. While the artistic quality of the city's statues varies, all were erected with good intentions and at considerable expense. This makes a ticklish diplomatic problem of the Department of Interior's efforts to ship some of them to what are called "more suitable locations," which really means—anywhere else!

CHURCH OF THE PRESIDENTS: At the northeast corner of Lafayette Park is St. John's Episcopal Church, the famous "Church of the Presidents." Pew number 54, on the left aisle, has been reserved for the President since 1816.

DOLLEY MADISON HOUSE, where the President's wife lived the last 12 years of her life, is east of the church, on the corner of Madison Place.

TRUXTON-DECATUR MUSEUM: West of the church, at 1610 H St., is the home of Stephen Decatur, hero of the naval wars against the Barbary pirates. A museum, which also honors Decatur's contemporary, Captain Thomas Truxton, traces American naval history in a series of exhibits that changes three times a year. **Open: 10:30 a.m. to 4 p.m., Tues. through Sun.**

BLAIR HOUSE, on Pennsylvania Ave., just west of Lafayette Park, is a guest house for notables visiting the President. It was built in 1810 and named for its owner, a political leader and Lincoln advisor.

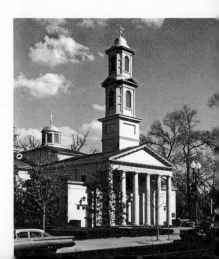

Left: Statue of Andrew Jackson was cast from cannon used in War of 1812. Right: St. John's was designed by architect Benjamin Latrobe while he was supervising construction of the Capitol. It is in the neoclassical style favored by the early 19th century, and has been the place of worship of at least ten Presidents.

Stretching 555 feet into the city's sky line is the slender marble shaft of the Washington Monument. It rests on a 41,341-ton base that extends 36 feet deep. Despite its height, it sways only one tenth of an inch in a 30-mile wind. Fifty flags, one for each state, encircle its base.

WASHINGTON MONUMENT CENTER OF MALL

This strikingly simple shaft of white marble serves a double purpose: as a distinctive memorial to a man of great character, and as a practical landmark for the confused traveler, who will never feel completely lost when he can see this giant obelisk on the Mall.

A marble monument to George Washington was proposed to Congress within a week after his death in 1799. While the legislators were in favor of the general idea, the only thing they could agree on was the marble. For almost 50 years they contemplated designs. Finally, a dramatic speech by Henry Clay sparked a spontaneous, nationwide money-raising campaign and Congress was prodded into action. On a sweltering Fourth of July afternoon in 1848, the cornerstone was laid while orators orated, women fainted from the heat, and a live American eagle perched high above the crowd on a temporary triumphal arch. The site had been chosen long before by Washington himself, but the modest hero had planned there a monument to the anonymous Revolutionary soldier.

Open: 8 a.m. to 11 p.m. daily, March 20 to Labor Day; 9 a.m. to 5 p.m. all other days. Closed Christmas Day.

The hollow square shaft, greatly simplified from architect Robert Mills' elaborate original design, went ahead at a good rate until it was 153 feet high. Inscribed memorial stones honoring Washington were sent from all over the world and inlaid on the inside wall. On the eve of the Civil War, however, construction stopped. Years went by, and the unfinished shaft sat forlornly, looking like a broken tooth. Finally, in 1876, Congress appropriated $200,000 to get the job done by the Army Corps of Engineers. Unfortunately, when work resumed again, the original marble could not be matched and to this day a distinct "high-water mark" is visible.

The monument was completed in 1884 and opened to the public two years later. Although a creation of the Victorian age and taste, the magnificently simple

Views from monument's top orient visitor, also graphically show layout of famous landmarks, often confusing from ground level (below, the White House).

memorial looks modern today. Its shape follows the classic ten to one proportion of ancient Egyptian obelisks, is 55 feet across at the base, and 555 feet high. Still the world's tallest masonry structure, it weighs 90,854 tons. It has settled less than one-thirtieth of an inch in the last 30 years.

A trip to the top takes only 70 seconds by elevator (price: ten cents, if you are nineteen or older), although in spring or summer there may be an hour's wait in line. Athletic types can avoid waiting by walking, but 898 steps make a long climb. Eight observation windows at the 500-foot level give a panoramic view of the city.

The monument is a fitting one, for the man it honors was likewise a dominant figure, yet simple and without pretension. George Washington was a quiet Virginia planter and soldier who inspired respect and confidence. He fought the Continental Congress for the troops and supplies he needed to pursue a war and improvised brilliantly with the little they gave him. In peacetime he resisted attempts to make him emperor or king, and helped establish the office of President as the democratic institution it remains.

OTHER MEMORIALS TO WASHINGTON: An equestrian statue is located on Pennsylvania Ave., at Washington Circle; another is on the grounds of the Washington Cathedral. A rather imperial seated statue, naked to the waist and draped in a Roman toga, is in the Smithsonian.

THE SYLVAN THEATRE, an outdoor amphitheater on the monument grounds, presents concerts and dance programs every Friday evening in June, July, and August. Phone REpublic 7-1820, Extension 2557, for current program.

LINCOLN MEMORIAL WEST END OF MALL

For the most dramatic sight in an impressive city, drive slowly past this classic structure late at night. Framed by huge Doric columns and illuminated by spotlights is a tall, brooding figure who seems to carry all the problems of a strife-torn nation on his shoulders.

This is the memorial to Abraham Lincoln in West Potomac Park. The site is appropriate. Lincoln liked to walk alone, late at night, from the White House to a spot near here, overlooking the black waters of the river. In the quiet darkness he sought answers to some of the most serious questions an American President ever had to face.

As in the case of the Washington Monument a half mile to the east, the strikingly beautiful memorial to Lincoln emerged from decades of petty bickering and intramural politics. Congress appointed the first of a series of commissions to plan a suitable memorial two years after Lincoln's tragic death. Various groups tried to raise money and design a monument, but none could get started. Not until 1901 was the present site selected by a Senate commission, which included it in a master plan for the entire District of Columbia. Congress, however, ignored both the master plan and the recommendations of a Fine Arts Council appointed by Theodore Roosevelt. Instead, it debated whether to build a memorial highway from Washington to Gettysburg or a monument at Union Station. Finally, it returned to the master plan and accepted the location on the banks of the Potomac, on a line drawn through the Capitol and the Washington Monument.

Open: 8 a.m. to midnight, daily.

Serene Lincoln Memorial is capital's most-visited site.

Once the site was chosen, the design for the memorial
—by architect Henry Bacon—was approved by Congress with little debate. On Memorial Day, 1922, the
memorial was dedicated by Chief Justice Taft.

The open-fronted building is white Colorado Yule
marble. It is 257 feet wide across the front and 187 feet
long. It stands nearly 80 feet high and is framed by 36
marble columns representing the states in the Union
that Lincoln had held together. Only the center col-
ums are perfectly vertical. The others tilt slightly in-
ward. This optical trick makes them appear straight.
If they were actually vertical they would seem to bulge
outward at the top.

The massive seated figure of Lincoln dominating the
interior chamber is the work of Daniel Chester French.
It is 19 feet high and carved from 28 blocks of white
Georgia marble, joined together without a noticeable
seam. The contemplative attitude of the figure is en-
hanced by illumination from above.

The interior walls are Indiana limestone, the interior
floor of pink Tennessee marble. High on each side wall
is an allegorical mural; below them, on the north wall, is
inscribed Lincoln's Second Inaugural Address, on the
south wall the few, imperishable words spoken at
Gettysburg cemetery in 1863.

FORD'S THEATRE AND THE HOUSE WHERE LINCOLN DIED

Ford's Theatre and the narrow house across the street from it were the scene of Abraham Lincoln's tragic end. Shortly after John Wilkes Booth fired his fatal shot at Ford's during the third act of a comedy called "Our American Cousin," on April 14, 1865, the President was tenderly carried to 516 10th St., N.W., the home of William Petersen, a tailor. There he died early the next morning. The house, now a national memorial, has been carefully restored to its original appearance. **Open: 9 a.m. to 5:30 p.m., Mon. through Sat.; 12:30 to 5:30 p.m., Sun. and holidays.**

The theatre, at 511 10th St., never opened again. It was divided into three stories and used to store government records. In 1893, tragedy struck again when the upper floors collapsed, killing 22 people. The unlucky structure now houses a large collection of Lincolniana. **Open: 9 a.m. to 9 p.m., Mon. through Sat.; 12:30 p.m. to 9 p.m. Sun.**

House where Lincoln died (left). Across street is Ford's Theatre, today a museum of Lincoln memorabilia, including earliest Brady portrait of 1860 (right).

JEFFERSON MEMORIAL

TIDAL BASIN, WEST POTOMAC PARK

Thomas Jefferson's memorial was dedicated by Franklin Delano Roosevelt on April 13, 1943, the 200th anniversary of Jefferson's birth, and stands in secluded West Potomac Park. Oddly enough, like the dome of the Capitol, erected during the Civil War, the Jefferson Memorial was completed while America was engaged in another bitter struggle—World War II—to ensure those freedoms which Jefferson had devoted his life to attaining and preserving. The architectural style of the memorial combines features of the Pantheon in Rome and Jefferson's own design for a rotunda at the University of Virginia, which he founded. The final plan, however, is the work of architects John Russell Pope, Otto R. Eggers, and Daniel P. Higgins.

Few men have been more dedicated to defining and protecting the rights of his fellow man than was Jefferson; his personal history gives testimony to this, and his memorial could not help but embody this spirit. On the pediment surmounting the portico, a sculptored group by Adolph A. Weinman reveals the 33-year old Jefferson reading his draft of the Declaration of Independence to the committee selected to draw up that document. Four panels inside recall memorable phrases from the Declaration and from other historical writings, including arguments for man's right to think and worship freely, the education of the common man by the state, and the necessity of keeping laws and institutions in step with changing times. High on the circular wall is still another memorable quotation from

Open: 8 a.m. to midnight, daily.

this great humanitarian: "I have sworn upon the altar of God eternal hostility against every form of tyranny over the mind of man."

The memorial's circular stone form is supported by 26 Ionic columns, 41 feet tall. Two types of marble were used in its construction: Vermont marble for the exterior, Georgia white marble for the interior. A massive dome crowns the building, its exterior rising 95 feet above the memorial's floor. Predominant in the building's great central chamber (86 feet in diameter) is a full-length bronze statue of Jefferson. Mounted on a six-foot pedestal of black Minnesota granite, the solemn figure stands 19 feet tall and looks toward the White House and the city Jefferson helped to design. Its sculptor, Rudulph Evans, won a $35,000 prize for the representation.

Nineteen-foot bronze statue of Jefferson is a favorite photographic subject. Jefferson himself was a man of wide interests. He kept weather records, collected fossils, checked all new inventions submitted to Patent Office. At right: Architect's drawing of the new John F. Kennedy Center for the Performing Arts.

JOHN F. KENNEDY CENTER FOR THE PERFORMING ARTS

East Bank of Potomac, Facing Theodore Roosevelt Island

This $45,000,000 theater complex for the performing arts is being erected on an 18-acre site near the Lincoln Memorial. As designed by architect Edward Durrell Stone, the center will be 630 feet long, 300 feet wide, and 100 feet high. It will house a 1,200-seat theater, a 2,750-seat symphony hall, and a 2,500-seat auditorium for opera, musical comedy, and ballet. A pavilion room will have two restaurants, an art gallery, and an area convertible to a theater in the round. There will be parking for 1,500 cars.

Magnolia (left) and
pink dogwood (above) are among
early spring blooms that
brighten the capital. Moderate
climate permits a wide
range of flowers and shrubs.

THE CHERRY BLOSSOMS

TIDAL BASIN

It's spring in Washington when the Japanese cherry trees bloom. The delicate blossoms follow the weather, not the calendar, but generally appear in early April and last for about two weeks. Approximately 600 of the beautiful trees are planted around the Tidal Basin, flanking the Jefferson Memorial. Most of them are a white type called Yoshino, which is the first to bloom. Just as the last delicate blossoms of the Yoshino are falling, another variety, the Kwanzan, starts producing thick clusters of rich pink double blossoms. A two-mile stretch of this variety is found in East Potomac Park (p. 128), south of the Tidal Basin. An annual festival in early April features a Cherry Blossom Princess from each state and territory and an elaborate pageant.

Delicate pink buds and white blossoms of Yoshino cherry trees add touch of enchantment to Tidal Basin during elaborate springtime festival.

In 1912, the city of Tokyo presented 3,000 cherry trees to the city of Washington as a gesture of friendship. People have strong feelings about them. When several dozen had to be removed to make way for the Jefferson Memorial, a group of women chained themselves to the trees in protest. On the afternoon of Pearl Harbor, another group did its bit for victory by chopping a number of them down. In 1952, the U.S. sent cuttings from the trees to their homeland to replace war-devastated nursery stocks. A grateful Japanese government sent in return an antique temple lantern.

Washington's magnolias bloom a little earlier than the cherry trees; dogwoods, azaleas, and rhododendrons a little later.

THE NATIONAL ARCHIVES

CONSTITUTION & 7th, N.W.

Imagine a row of 150,000 four-drawer file cabinets. This is the amount of storage space the National Archives requires to hold the permanent records of the U.S. government. In fireproof vaults with automatically controlled temperature and humidity, the National Archives and Records Service preserves treaties, records of the Land Office and the Census Bureau, and all other papers that must be kept for legal or historic reasons. (Any government agency seeking to thin out its files must obtain permission from the Archives.)

The most precious items in the Archives' care are on permanent display in the Exhibition Hall. Here, sealed in glass-and-bronze cases, are the Declaration of Independence, the Constitution, and the Bill of Rights. They are mechanically lowered each night into a reinforced, shockproof, fireproof, safe.

Open: 9 a.m. to 10 p.m., Mon. through Sat.; 1 p.m. to 10 p.m., Sun. and holidays.

Corinthian columns of National Archives building (left) make its classic exterior one of city's finest. Massive bronze doors lead to marble Exhibition Hall (right), where Declaration of Independence and other historic documents are displayed.

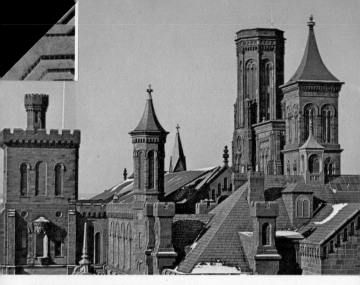

Original Smithsonian building was designed by
James Renwick in 1848 and completed in 1852. Within are editorial
and administrative offices, and National Herbarium.

SMITHSONIAN INSTITUTION THE MALL

On the south side of the Mall, between the Capitol and
the Washington Monument, stands a towered and
turreted red-sandstone castle well over a century old.
Diagonally across the way from it is a brand new structure of tremendous size and striking modern design.
Both of these, plus five other buildings in architectural
styles ranging from oversized Quonset hut to Florentine
Renaissance palace, are part of the Smithsonian
Institution, keeper of the world's largest and most
varied collection of materials in the fields of history,
art, technology, and the natural sciences.
All buildings open: 9 a.m. to 4:30 p.m., daily.

James Smithson, a lonely British scientist, who was the illegitimate son of a Duke of Northumberland, died in 1829, leaving an unusual and far-reaching will. He bequeathed to the United States, a country he had never seen, a fortune "to found at Washington, under the name of the Smithsonian Institution, an establishment for the increase and diffusion of knowledge among men." The terms of his will gave a nephew the right to use the money during his lifetime. Some $5,500,000 was left in 1829. The nephew died in 1835 leaving about $500,000. After ten years of discussion in Congress about whether or not to accept a foreign gift, Joseph Henry, one of America's top scientists, was appointed to head the project. He served as secretary of the Institution for 32 years (1846–1878), was responsible for its broad interest in practically every branch of scientific endeavor. It sponsored the publication of scientific papers, provided money grants and apparatus for original research, and ran the first of more than 2,000 field expeditions.

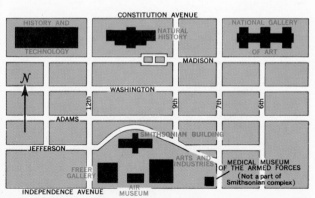

Spencer Baird, the second secretary, greatly expanded the Institution's activities by training young scientists and sending them along on government expeditions during the period of westward expansion. It was largely on Baird's recommendation that the U.S. purchased Alaska from Russia in 1867. Baird knew of the territory's wealth of natural resources from the Smithsonian's geological explorations there.

Shortly before the turn of the century, the great collections that now fill the exhibition halls were begun. At the same time, the museum's interests, formerly confined to science and natural history, were broadened to include fine arts and American history.

The rambling old Arts and Industries Building was completed in 1882 and the present Natural History Building added in 1910. The Freer Gallery opened in 1923 and the magnificent National Gallery in 1941. The new Museum of History and Technology was completed in 1964.

Plaster model for bronze statue of Freedom atop Capitol dome stands in central hall of Arts and Industries Building. Other exhibits are being shifted (over eight-year period) to new Museum of History and Technology on opposite page.

More than 52,000,000 items are stored in the Smithsonian's seven buildings. Only a small portion of these are on display, but it has been estimated that if a visitor spent one minute on every object on public exhibition, he would need two and a half years to see them all. On a first visit, the discriminating viewer will do well to check a floor plan at the entrance to each building, and try to see only the things he is most interested in.

The most popular exhibits are two airplanes. A figure of Orville Wright clings to the wing of the frail and primitive craft that first carried man aloft in powered flight, at Kitty Hawk, North Carolina, in 1903. It stayed up just 12 seconds and flew a distance of only 120 feet, but on that brisk December morning were born today's mighty jet airliners and tomorrow's rockets. Just behind the Wright brothers' tiny aircraft hangs a small silver monoplane named the "Spirit of St. Louis." Only 27 feet long, it carried Charles A. Lindbergh from New York to Paris, nonstop, in May of 1927.

Gowns worn by wives of United States Presidents are exhibited in period settings in First Ladies Hall. Figure (left) shows 19th-century elegance of Mary Todd Lincoln. Elsewhere tourists can view early appliances, such as sewing machine (above, right) and changing character of American military uniforms (above, left) from Revolution to present.

During the past few years, much of the historical material from the old Arts and Industries Building has been moved to modern display halls in the new Museum of History and Technology. Among these items are George Washington's surveying instruments and his uniform of buff and blue. The flag that Francis Scott Key, peering through the haze of battle during the War of 1812, saw waving over Fort McHenry now hangs in the Rotunda to remind us of the incident that resulted in our national anthem; it is over 42 feet high, has 15 stripes. A colonial mahogany highboy contrasts with the simple portable desk on which Jefferson drafted the Declaration of Independence. Nearby are the plain pine table and chairs used by Grant and Lee at Appomattox Court House.

Alan Shepard, Jr.'s Freedom 7,
America's first
manned space vehicle,
has position of honor in
Air Museum. Tiny
Bell X-1 (below, right),
flown by Air Force Captain
Charles Yeager in
1947, was first jet
to break sonic barrier.

THE AIR MUSEUM

A low, arch-roofed temporary building sits squeezed into
the space between the old Arts and Industries Building
and the Freer Gallery, facing Independence Ave. The Air
Museum plans in 1971 to have new quarters large
enough to display its historic planes under one roof, but
for the present it has to make do with one small structure that looks like a Quonset hut. Outside stand tall,
shiny rockets and missiles, posing incongruously against
the nearby red stone turrets of the original Smithsonian
"castle." All famous aircraft, including the "Kitty Hawk
Flyer" and "Spirit of St. Louis" which are now in the old
Arts and Industries Building or stored in hangars and
warehouses all over the country, belong to the Air Museum. Eventually they will be brought together in a single
comprehensive exposition of the history of flight.

Meanwhile, some extremely well-designed exhibits in the present tiny building do a graphic job of exploring the same subject on a smaller scale, aided by models and realistic dioramas. Displays of simple aircraft instruments and pilots' crude personal equipment used on famous early flights point up the amazing aeronautical advances made in a relatively short time. Recent rocket nose cones and space capsules stand close to the first plane (built by the Wright brothers) to complete a cross-country flight. It took 80 days back in 1911 and advertised a soft drink en route! With advances almost daily in the exploration of space, the staff of this museum must work continuously to keep up to date.

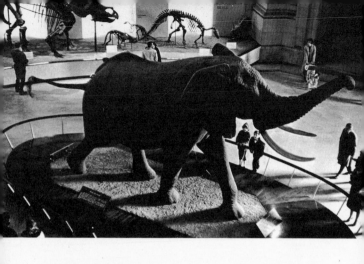

MUSEUM OF NATURAL HISTORY

Elephants, Indians, and Eskimos are grouped with a collection of fine arts, a million-dollar diamond, and a 70-foot dinosaur in this museum's melange of natural and man-made wonders.

The art collection doesn't belong in a museum otherwise devoted to nature and primitive man, but the terms of the bequest keep it out of the National Gallery. So here it waits in cramped quarters until it gets a building of its own. The famous Hope diamond fits rightfully into the Hall of Gems and Minerals, one of the world's finest collections. This exciting new gallery is an example of the dramatic display techniques being used to gradually update all branches of the Smithsonian. The dinosaur comes from Utah, is 135,000,000 years old and a vegetarian. It took seven years to free his bones from the rock matrix encasing them.

Twelve-ton bull elephant
(left), largest on
record, guards museum
rotunda. Dioramas in Hall of
Fossil Invertebrates
show underwater life of
early geologic eras. Below:
Ordovician period.
Outstanding in modernized
Hall of Gems and
Minerals is famous
Hope diamond (right).

Even larger than the entrance-hall elephant is a 92-foot-long blue whale in the Hall of the Oceanic Life. The whale is made of plastic, while the elephant is (or was) real and required the services of two taxidermists for nearly two years to mount his hide. Insects are a lot easier to prepare for exhibition than mammals, which is fortunate, since the museum owns some 14,000,000 of them, plus 10,000,000 mollusks, 3,000,000 fishes and marine invertebrates, and 500,000 birds. Out of this tremendous collection the generous Smithsonian has distributed many thousands of its specimens to schools and colleges across the nation.

Life in early America is portrayed in six period rooms (including an entire late 17th century Massachusetts Bay Colony house) and 50 displays in a new second floor hall that dramatically exhibits clothing, weapons, furniture, and domestic arts of colonial times.

Indian family groups include some leftover models from the Chicago Columbian Exposition of 1893, but still seem realistic enough to lend credibility to the story of the irate woman who angrily wrote her congressman to complain of the Smithsonian's inhuman practice of stuffing real Indians! Another section of Anthropology Hall uses the most modern exhibition styling to show weird animal-like dance masks from Alaska, eerily glowing in a darkened corner. The Smithsonian started its studies of native Indian tribes when the western territories were first opened and has had its scientists in the field ever since. Major John Wesley Powell, the intrepid one-armed explorer of the Grand Canyon of the Colorado, organized the museum's Bureau of American Ethnology in 1879. At the time its studies were restricted to living Indians, but today archaeology forms a large part of the program.

Hopi snake dancers are most realistic of main-floor Indian and Eskimo habitat groups that depict primitive cultures from the Arctic to Tierra del Fuego. Mountain lion (or puma), shown in authentic Yellowstone Canyon setting, is part of Natural History Museum's Hall of North American Mammals.

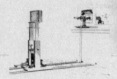

BREVET LT. COL. J. J. WOODWARD, CHIEF OF THE MEDICAL AND MICROSCOPIC SECTION OF THE MUSEUM (1864) PRODUCED SOME OF THE EARLIEST PHOTOMICROGRAPHS MADE IN THIS COUNTRY.

Medical Museum exhibit shows pioneer photomicrography of 1864. Special Smithsonian exhibits are changed regularly, often sent on tour. Typical are George Catlin's Indian portraits at right, painted in the 1830's.

SPECIAL EXHIBITS are featured regularly at all branches of the Smithsonian, often with a dozen or more going on at once among the seven buildings. Material for these shows sometimes comes from the museum's own collections, sometimes is borrowed from other institutions.

NATIONAL COLLECTION OF FINE ARTS, a changing collection, and **NATIONAL PORTRAIT GALLERY,** a collection of statues and paintings of historic Americans, is in the former Patent Office Building on G Street at 8th, N.W.

THE SMITHSONIAN LIBRARY contains working collections of 500,000 volumes maintained at branches of the Institution for immediate reference, plus more than 1,000,000 publications at the Library of Congress.

THE INTERNATIONAL EXCHANGE SERVICE supervises world-wide swapping of more than 1,000,000 books, articles, and technical papers annually.

DIVISION OF RADIATION AND ORGANISMS, located in the original Smithsonian building, does basic research on photosynthesis, photobiology, and radiant energy.

ASTROPHYSICAL OBSERVATORY, established in 1891 to measure infrared solar rays, now studies meteors, cosmic rays, radio communication, missile guidance; has 12 satellite tracking stations around the world.

NATIONAL ZOOLOGICAL PARK, see pp. 116-117.

MEDICAL MUSEUM of the Armed Forces Institute of Pathology is on Independence Ave., between 7th and 8th Sts., east of the Smithsonian buildings.

THE FREER GALLERY OF ART

While the Smithsonian has received many gifts of doubtful artistic value, it has been unusually lucky in its major legacies. One of the finest is the Freer Gallery collection of Oriental art, donated by Detroit industrialist Charles L. Freer.

The gallery, opened in 1923, is in the style of a Florentine Renaissance palace. It has 19 exhibition halls around an open court and stands just southwest of the original Smithsonian "castle."

In spite of little formal education, Freer was a man of discrimination and taste. He retired at 44, a wealthy man (he had started working at 14), and devoted the last two decades of his life to his collection. Originally interested in etchings and lithographs by American artists, he went on to Japanese prints, screen paintings, and sculpture, then to the art of Asia and the Near East. On exhibition are selections from more than 10,000 pieces gathered in China, Japan, Korea, India, Iran, Egypt, and Syria. In addition, there are early Christian paintings and Biblical manuscripts in Greek, Aramaic, and Armenian that draw scholars to the museum from all over the world. Freer himself, on a trip through the Near East, came across the precious manuscripts almost accidentally when they were offered for sale by a wandering Arab.

While the Oriental collection predominates, several of the galleries are devoted to western painters such as Winslow Homer, John Singer Sargent, and Albert Ryder. Freer's favorite American artist was James Whistler, and the gallery owns the greatest collection of his work. One hall is devoted to Whistler's "Peacock

Wooden Japanese guardian figure is from Kamakura period, 1200 A.D.

Room,'' an unusual decorating project created by the artist for a London shipbuilder. It was later dismantled and recreated at the gallery.

Excellent reproductions of many of the museum's finest Oriental art works are on sale at nominal prices. **Open: 9 a.m. to 4:30 p.m., daily except Christmas.**

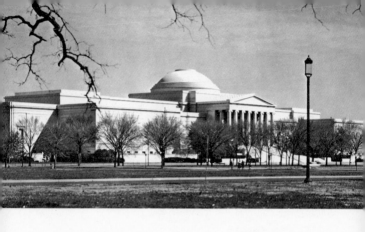

The magnificent painting on the preceding pages is one of the world's great works of art. As such it belongs in one of the world's fine galleries, which should be located where a maximum number of people can visit and appreciate it. Fortunately, that's just where Botticelli's "Adoration of the Magi" rests—in Washington's National Gallery of Art, along with more than 27,000 other paintings, sculptures, drawings, and prints.

The gallery has more than 500,000 square feet of floor space. Its exterior is of a pale, rose-white Tennessee marble (to minimize glare). In the rain it turns a lovely pink. From the main entrance on the Mall the visitor steps into a huge rotunda supported by 24 Ionic columns of dark green Italian marble. In contrast to the dark and formal rotunda, the paintings are displayed in 90 intimate, well-lit galleries. On a lower level are 20 more galleries for drawings and sculpture.

Open: 10 a.m. to 5 p.m., Mon. through Sat., except Christmas and New Year's; 2 to 10 p.m., Sun.

Massive but simply designed National Gallery of Art (left) houses some of world's finest works of art. Collection of sculpture and French tapestries distinguishes its West Hall (right). Earliest paintings begin in rooms to left of hall, while the far end opens into garden court where free public concerts are given on Sundays.

Andrew Mellon was a Pittsburgh industrialist and steel tycoon, and Secretary of the Treasury from 1921 to 1932 under Presidents Harding, Coolidge, and Hoover. An active interest in art started Mellon collecting at an early age. He had excellent taste. Most of his later important purchases were made under the guidance of famed art dealer Joseph Duveen, who specialized in bringing together the finest European paintings and the largest American fortunes.

Mellon's outstanding purchase was made in 1930, when the Soviet government, strapped for cash, sold him 21 masterpieces from its renowned Hermitage Gallery. One of these alone, Raphael's "Alba Madonna," cost more than $1,000,000.

In 1937, Mellon had architect John Russell Pope design the massive but beautifully simple National Gallery building and bequeathed it, along with his entire collection, to the people of the United States. The gallery is under the administration of the Smithsonian.

91

Surveys of National
Gallery visitors rate these
three paintings among
all-time favorites. Large
portrait of "The Skater"
(opposite page), done in
subtle, dark colors of
a wintry afternoon,
is work of Gilbert Stuart.
Below: Moody shadows add
drama and depth to
Rembrandt's "The Philosopher."
Its dark tones contrast
sharply with vivid colors
in Renoir's "Girl with
Watering Can."

Unfortunately, Andrew Mellon did not live to see his generous gift finished in 1941. The building cost $15,000,000 and Mr. Mellon added $5,000,000 for upkeep. Ignoring the natural inclination to put his own name on this munificent bequest, Mellon insisted from the beginning that it be called simply the National Gallery. Always a canny one, he figured the lack of personal identification would bring other bequests to the great museum. He was right. Even before the building was completed, Samuel H. Kress, founder of the five-and-ten-cent store chain, donated his entire collection, one of the finest in private hands. Soon afterward, Joseph E. Widener gave his famous group of paintings, sculpture, and decorative arts. Chester Dale, besides many outright gifts, placed a number of fine modern paintings on indefinite loan. (The National Gallery, like the Louvre, includes no paintings in the permanent collection by artists dead less than 20 years.) Once these major donations had made the museum one of the world's finest, dozens of other bequests came in. New paintings are constantly being acquired.

On a first visit, the best way to get acquainted is to take the 45-minute lecture tour, starting at 11 a.m. or 3 p.m. If you prefer a do-it-yourself tour, start at Gallery 1 in the west wing and follow the numbers for a chronological trip that ranges from the 13th to 20th centuries. For 25 cents you can rent an earplug radio that receives a running lecture in each gallery.

The paintings start with the early Italian school, some over 600 years old. Their brilliant colors and gold leaf still glow brightly. This style is followed by the more naturalistic work of Botticelli, Raphael, and others of their period.

Gallery visitor cranes for better view of Matisse odalisque. Child's stroller is provided free by the gallery, as are wheel chairs when needed.

Flemish and German works include detailed religious scenes and grandiose portraits by Rubens and Van Dyck, contrasting with simple Dutch landscapes and scenes of everyday life. Two entire galleries are devoted to paintings by Rembrandt. Frivolous and gay French paintings of the 18th century contrast with the formal, aloof British portraits of the same period. Early American portraits show leading colonial citizens.

Some of the most popular galleries are those of the impressionists and postimpressionists—Degas, Renoir, Cezanne, Monet; also Gauguin, Van Gogh, Toulouse-Lautrec. Later American paintings include seascapes by Winslow Homer and works by James McNeill Whistler, John Singer Sargent, Albert Pinkham Ryder, and George Bellows.

Modern French paintings on long-term loan to the museum fill four galleries containing outstanding examples of the work of Picasso, Braque, Modigliani, Matisse, and others. Salvador Dali's large and unusual rendition of "The Last Supper" has a room to itself, is a favorite among gallery visitors.

Hand-held cameras are permitted in the galleries.

95

On the lower floor are galleries containing Flemish tapestries, Renaissance furniture, jewelry, bronzes, stained-glass windows, and 18th century French furniture and tapestries. Also here are 22,000 prints, drawings, and etchings dating from the 15th century to the present, decorative arts, pre-Columbian sculpture—and an excellent cafeteria.

Also on the lower floor is the Index of American Design, an invaluable reference source of 15,000 water colors and 5,000 photographs depicting popular arts of the U.S. from 1700 to 1900.

Left: "Breezing Up," seascape by Winslow Homer. Early Picasso (above) called "The Lovers" is one of many modern paintings on loan to gallery. Below: "Fatata te Miti," a Gauguin vision of Tahiti.

Corcoran boasts two Stuart portraits of Washington.

CORCORAN GALLERY

17th & E, N.W.

Before there was a National Gallery, the Corcoran was Washington's leading art museum. Although now overshadowed, it is a handsome building containing some outstanding works of art, especially those of American artists from colonial times to the present.

It was founded by William W. Corcoran, a Washington banker so wealthy that he bought up the entire bond issue that financed the Mexican War. (His Lafayette Square mansion, bought from Daniel Webster, is now the site of the Chamber of Commerce.)

The Corcoran Gallery's entrance on 17th St. is flanked by two unusual bronze lions, duplicates of a pair found in St. Peter's in Rome. The gallery itself is white marble. Its most interesting paintings are the early American portraits. Since these are on the second floor, start your tour there and work down.

Most of the portraits are by distinguished artists such as John Singleton Copley, Rembrandt Peale, and Gilbert Stuart. Visitors often wonder why the Corcoran has two original Stuart portraits of Washington that are almost exact duplicates. The answer is that the artist made more than 70 known copies of this famous picture (it's the one on the $1 bill). He often referred to it as his emergency "hundred-dollar bill," since he could always find a customer for another.

Don't miss Samuel F. B. Morse's 7-by-11-foot painting of "The Old House of Representatives." Although not a masterpiece, it contains 86 portraits and is a fascinatingly detailed look at a Congress of the 1820's.

Later American works at the Corcoran include landscapes by artists of the Hudson River school. The 20th century is represented by George Bellows, Edward Hopper, Raphael Soyer, and John Marin.

The gallery has an active concert and classic-film schedule, and is internationally known for its major biennial exhibits and traveling shows. **Open: 10 a.m. to 4:30 p.m., Tues. through Fri.; 9 a.m. to 4:30 p.m., Sat.; 2 p.m. to 5 p.m., Sun. and holidays.**

DAUGHTERS OF THE AMERICAN REVOLUTION: The DAR headquarters, north of the Pan American Union on 17th St., has a museum of historical items, such as John Paul Jones' spectacles, John Hancock's desk, and Revolutionary War flags. **Open: 10 a.m. to 3 p.m., Mon. through Fri.**

AMERICAN RED CROSS: The headquarters building on 17th St., between the DAR and the Corcoran, has a basement museum showing the history of the Red Cross from the Civil War period to the present. **Open: 9 a.m. to 4 p.m., Mon. through Fri.**

Patio (left) brings
tropical atmosphere to lobby
of Pan American Union.
Right: Union's OAS Council
Chamber. Commemorative statue
of South American liberator
Simón Bolívar (above) stands in
park adjoining building.

PAN AMERICAN UNION

17th & CONSTITUTION, N.W.

This handsome marble building, sometimes called the
House of the Americas, is now the permanent headquarters of the Organization of American States. The
OAS is charged with maintaining the peace, freedom,
and security of the 21 republics of the Western Hemi-
sphere. It meets in an impressive modern Council
Chamber whose seats are equipped with earphones for
simultaneous interpretation in English, Spanish,
French, and Portuguese. Thus it carries on the spirit of
the original Pan American Union, which was formed in
1889 to improve inter-American relations.

Visitors entering the building's main entrance step
into a Latin-American patio. Water plays in a pink marble fountain and palm trees arch overhead under a
sliding glass roof that is open to the sky in warm

weather. A bookstore and arts-and-crafts shop are also on the main floor, as well as an art gallery displaying the works of artists of all the republics.

On the second floor, a Hall of Heroes overlooks the patio. Here are the flags of the OAS members and busts of prominent men in their history. The adjacent Hall of the Americas is 100 feet long and 65 feet wide, has Tiffany crystal chandeliers and stained-glass windows. It is used for diplomatic banquets, concerts, and receptions.

Visitors can browse or have the free services of a guide. Ask to see the underground corridor connecting with the annex a block away. Its walls are covered by a three-dimensional mural ablaze with tropical colors. **Open: 8:30 a.m. to 4 p.m., Mon. through Sat.**

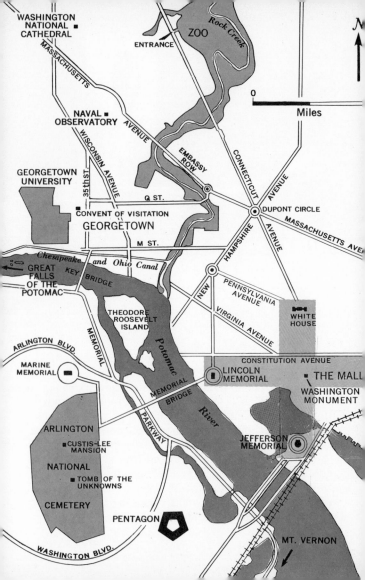

BEYOND THE CITY'S CENTER

Visitors with the time or inclination to travel beyond the city's center will find other fascinating Washingtons to explore. The map opposite shows several of them.

Northwest of the White House, in the fashionable and historic community of Georgetown, there is a residential Washington. Adjacent to it, just across the Bridge of Buffaloes, is so-called Embassy Row, where many of the foreign legations are located. There are museums to see in this area, historic houses, and, out Massachusetts Ave., the great Washington Cathedral and the Naval Observatory.

Washington Out-of-Doors begins at Rock Creek Park, an area of picnic and playgrounds, hikes and horseback riding, bird watching and garden walking. Within striking distance are the Chesapeake & Ohio Canal and the Great Falls of the Potomac, and for nature lovers unspoiled Theodore Roosevelt Island.

The island is part of a third Washington—that of the life along the Potomac river front. Golf, tennis, swimming, boating, concerts, and other entertainments are all available at the water's edge.

The next 28 pages will take you in a logical sequence through these areas of the District that lie beyond official, downtown Washington. Some of the sights and activities are of specialized interest, some are seasonal, but most have general appeal the year around— and can be reached on public transportation.

For the areas outside Washington, see the map on p. 143 and the pages following it. These contain information on sights across the Potomac and as far south as Mount Vernon.

Typical Georgetown home is three windows wide and made of brick. Hallmarks of early Federal period architecture are the fanlight over the door and the long lintel stones over the windows. About a quarter of Georgetown's houses were built more than 150 years ago.

GEORGETOWN

The most exclusive residential district in Washington is this "city within a city" located only a mile and a half northwest of the White House. Cosmopolitan little Georgetown is about ten blocks square, and is the home of more notables in "Who's Who" than any area of comparable size in the U.S.

Named for George II of England (not George Washington), Georgetown was a thriving seaport for the tobacco trade for 40 years before being included in the area chosen for the capital. It lived graciously, and early Washingtonians sought relief from the crudities of the "Federal City" in its civilized society. Eventually, the harbor silted up, large ships could not enter, and Georgetown lost importance as a port. It tried a commercial comeback as the eastern terminus of the Ches-

Dumbarton House, an 1800 mansion on 28th and Q Sts., is distinguished for the role it played in the War of 1812. This was the place to which Dolley Madison fled with state papers and a portrait of Washington when the British burned the White House in 1814.

apeake & Ohio Canal, but the new Baltimore & Ohio Railroad paralleled its route and took most of the traffic. The area ran downhill and became almost a slum. After World War II, however, its proximity to the center of the city spurred a revival. Old houses were remodeled, new ones built in the old style.

The best way to see Georgetown is to park your car and walk along the old brick sidewalks lined with Federal style (1790–1820) houses. Wisconsin Ave. runs through its center and is the shopping district. It features small bookstores, antique and gift shops. Picturesque brick homes on the side streets feature brightly colored doorways, brass knockers, and old gas lamps. Picket fences shield attractive little flower gardens and shaded patios.

All kinds of people live in Georgetown, ranging from the very wealthy to groups of secretaries who pool their salaries to afford the rental of a little house. (John F. Kennedy was a Georgetown resident while a senator.)

For curious visitors who would like a glimpse behind Georgetown's shutters and fences, there is an annual spring house tour on the first weekend in April and a garden tour on the third. For information, call the Georgetown Historical Society.

DUMBARTON HOUSE, at 28th and Q Sts., has been lovingly restored by the Colonial Dames of America. **Open: 10 a.m. to 5 p.m., Mon. through Sat.**

BARGE TRIPS ON THE C. & O. CANAL start at the wharf near 30th and M Sts. (pp. 122–123).

GEORGETOWN UNIVERSITY: The 100-acre campus of the oldest Catholic university in the U.S. (founded 1789) lies between Reservoir and Canal Rds. on the western edge of Georgetown. In addition to highly regarded law and medical schools, there is a Center for Strategic Studies for research on national growth and responsible use of national power.

Street sign (right) conforms to Georgetown's early 19th-century style of architecture. Tall shuttered doors with fanlights (top, left) and decorative wrought iron rail seen in shadow on doorstep (top, right) add to town's charm, as do old brick sidewalks and soft glow of gaslight (left) illuminating many entranceways.

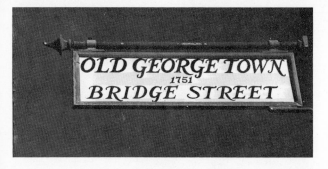

Most embassies can be identified by a colorful
escutcheon above the doorway. Above are national seals
of Thailand (left), the Philippines (top, right) and
Sweden. Bridge of Buffaloes, guarded by
bronze figures, connects Georgetown
with Embassy Row via Q St., N.W.

No muezzin chants from the balcony of this minaret above the Islamic Center. His ancient figure has been replaced by a modern tape recorder. Note too that the façade of the mosque is not parallel to building's exterior. The mosque has been built on an angle so that it faces the Holy City of Mecca, while Center, which houses the Islamic Institute, faces Massachusetts Ave. Hours: 1 to 6 p.m., Mon. through Wed.; 1 to 5 p.m., Fri.; 10 a.m. to 5 p.m., Sat. and Sun. Each Fri. at noon (1 p.m. E.D.T.) there is a service open to the public.

EMBASSY ROW

Dupont Circle, or as near to it on Massachusetts Ave. as you could get, was the most fashionable address in Washington at the turn of the century. The country's newly made millionaires, descending on the capital to socialize and do a bit of politicking, built dozens of grandiose mansions in this section. Some have now been torn down, others belong to schools or exclusive private clubs, and many have been purchased by foreign governments, who find them ideal embassies. Most of them are in the formal or elaborate architectural styles of an earlier day, but several are contemporary and in the character of the countries they represent.

National emblem of Venezuela.

Lions guard British embassy.

Sacred lion and shah's crown mark door of Iranian embassy.

For an interesting walk or drive along Embass[y], start at Scott Circle (15th & N) and follow Mas[sachu]setts Ave. northwest for a mile and a half. [In the] stretch alone more than two dozen embassies and legations are identified by their flags or escutcheons.

At the Islamic Center (which you can't miss) turn right on Belmont Road to Kalorama Circle and the adjacent side streets for a look at the French, Finnish, Ethiopian, and Thai embassies, among others.

Embassy open house is held each spring on the second Saturday in May, with six countries participating and serving refreshments typical of their native land. Since the host countries rotate yearly, check with the U.S. Department of State for specific schedules.

(Other embassies are clustered near Meridian Hill Park, off 16th St., N.W.)

THE PHILLIPS COLLECTION, which is located in a stately old brick town house at 21st and Q Sts. (two blocks east of the Bridge of Buffaloes), is a truly impressive collection of modern art. It starts with El Greco, Goya, and Corot, and proceeds through Cezanne, Matisse, and Van Gogh to Braque, Roualt, and Pollock. Free concerts are given on Sunday afternoons and Monday evenings. **Open: 11 a.m. to 6 p.m., Tues. through Sat.; 2 to 7 p.m., Sun.; 11 a.m. to 10 p.m., Mon.; closed July 4, Labor Day, and Christmas.**

WASHINGTON GALLERY OF MODERN ART, 1502 21st St., N.W., a block from the Phillips, is newest of the city's museums, specializes in major exhibitions of present-day artists. Phone for exhibit information.

HOWARD UNIVERSITY, 6th & Euclid Sts., was founded in 1867 to help educate the newly freed Negroes. Student body and faculty are now multiracial.

Despite scaffolding
and aura of incompleteness,
Cathedral of St. Peter
and St. Paul is
impressive. It is
being built stone on stone
(no steel framework)
as were medieval
cathedrals. Carved blocks
of limestone may be
purchased and donated by
visitors. Left: Ervin
Bossanyi expresses war and
destruction in unusual
stained-glass window. Statue
of Washington (above, far
right), in gilded bronze,
is at cathedral's
south entrance, at foot of
Pilgrim Steps.

WASHINGTON CATHEDRAL

WISCONSIN & MASSACHUSETTS AVES., N.W.

Atop Mount St. Alban, the highest point in the District of Columbia (400 feet), a tremendous 14th-century Gothic structure is rising. This is the Cathedral of St. Peter and St. Paul, begun in 1907 and now about 70 per cent complete. More familiarly known as Washington (or National) Cathedral, it is being built in the medieval manner, stone on stone, without a steel framework. But a modern touch is the radiant-heating system installed under the marble floor.

Although Protestant Episcopal in administration, its three daily services are nonsectarian and the church has no regular local congregation. Chapels in the cathedral have been temporary homes for Russian Orthodox, Polish Catholic, and Jewish groups.

Woodrow Wilson is buried in the third bay of the south outer aisle, Admiral George Dewey in the Bethlehem Chapel. The Bishop's Garden is a beautiful one; it can be entered from the south aisle of the crypt.

ROCK CREEK PARK

Rock Creek Park includes 3,400 acres, of which 1,800 are in the District of Columbia (the remaining 1,600 in the park's continuation in Maryland). It is an area of woodland glades, open meadows, hiking trails, and bridle paths. Rock Creek itself is 12 miles long. The stretch immediately above its inlet to the Potomac serves as the boundary between Georgetown and the rest of Washington. Farther upstream, along the Rock Creek & Potomac Parkway, it courses through the zoo, then heads northward through the Park.

Rock Creek Park was created by Congress in 1890.

When outdoorsman Theodore Roosevelt was President, he enjoyed long hikes through its woods.

Pierce Mill, just north of the zoo, is one of eight mills formerly situated along the creek. No longer in operation, it still remains a fine example of a 19th century, water-powered mill. **Open: Fri., 9 a.m. to 5 p.m., September 1 to June 16; Sat., 9 a.m. to 5 p.m., June 16 to August 31; Sun., 1 p.m. to 5 p.m., the year around.**

Picnic grounds with fireplaces are generously spaced along Beach Dr., which follows Rock Creek through the park, except for its northernmost three miles (which consequently are less crowded). The Trail Center, on Beach Dr. off Military Rd., near the eastern entrance, is the junction of an extensive system of hiking trails and has a ranger on duty to supply information.

Edgewater Stables, under the Taft Bridge on Rock Creek Parkway, rents and boards horses and gives riding lessons. Phone: ADams 4-9664.

Weekend activities in the open fields of Washington's parks run the gamut from small-fry baseball games to falconry.

Washington's relatively mild climate supports a rich
variety of wild flowers, particularly in Rock Creek Park in
spring when (left to right) wild violets, trillium, and columbines
appear. Polar bear from the Arctic and rosy
pelican from Africa (opposite page) are among residents of zoo.

WASHINGTON'S ZOO began when the Smithsonian
acquired a herd of buffalo. The animals were kept in a
pen on the Mall, and as the White House received exotic wildlife gifts from abroad more pens were added.
Finally something had to be done, and in 1890 a
National Zoological Park was established in Rock Creek
Park. A circus stranded in town donated two elephants
and soon the new zoo found itself swamped with free
animals. It now rates among the world's finest, has
sponsored international expeditions to "bring 'em back
alive," and developed new techniques to keep animals
healthy on arrival. Among the most popular recent
guests are a happy pair of pigmy hippos (who regularly
produce offspring that make fine material for trades
with other zoos) and an excellent collection of bears.

The zoo's main entrance is located in the 3000 block
of Connecticut Ave.
**The grounds are open daily from dawn to dark, the
buildings from 9 a.m. to 5 p.m.**

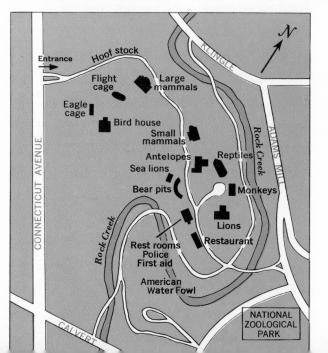

Entrance

Hoof stock

Flight cage

Large mammals

KLINGLE

N

Eagle cage

Bird house

Small mammals

Rock Creek

ADAMS MILL

Antelopes

Reptiles

Sea lions

CONNECTICUT AVENUE

Bear pits

Monkeys

Lions

Rest rooms
Police
First aid

Restaurant

Rock Creek

American
Water Fowl

NATIONAL
ZOOLOGICAL
PARK

CALVERT

Rock Creek Nature Center uses modern techniques to exhibit and explain secrets of nature to adults as well as youngsters (left). Visiting ballet groups from United States and abroad perform in open-air Carter Barron Amphitheater (above). There classical and modern productions alternate to fill evenings from early June through Labor Day.

BRINGING NATURE INDOORS and the theater out-doors are two more of the many activities at Rock Creek. A splendid new Nature Center, located off Military Rd., on the park's west side, exhibits the flora and fauna of the area, also houses a small but very fine planetarium, which has showings on weekends and Wednesday and Friday afternoons. A self-guiding trail close by provides further insight into nature's wonders, and Saturday programs for children are conducted by park naturalists. Phone REpublic 7-1820, Ext. 638, for schedules.

Top entertainment takes place nightly from early June through Labor Day at the Carter Barron Amphitheater. Road companies of Broadway musicals, jazz and ballet festivals, and symphony concerts are featured evenings at 8:30 at this open-air theater in the park near Colorado Ave. and 16th St., N.W.

For program information write: Director, National Capital Region, NPS., Dept. of the Interior, Washington 25, D.C.

GREAT FALLS OF THE POTOMAC

One of the East's fine scenic wonders is almost unknown. Because of Washington's other more convenient attractions, the Great Falls of the Potomac River, a scant 12 miles away, are generally overlooked. The river itself begins in the heart of the Alleghenies, some 200 miles to the northwest. At Great Falls it has turned into a powerful stream over a quarter mile wide and 50 feet deep. The river brings seeds from west of the mountains, and a profusion of wild flowers grows along its banks. In the spring redbud and flowering dogwood

At full spring flood 480,000 cubic feet of water pass over Great Falls each second, a volume surpassing Niagara's normal flow. Bridge over deep gorge (left) on Maryland side lets visitors overhang rushing spring waters, while observation deck at end of three-quarter-mile walk commands view across main course of river (right). Park on far side, in Virginia, may be reached via five mile extension at the northern end of the George Washington Memorial Parkway.

brighten large parks on both sides of the falls. On the Maryland side, the restored Great Falls Tavern of 1830, once a rest stop on the Chesapeake & Ohio Canal, is now a museum with displays of canal history and local wildlife. **(Hours are 10 a.m. to 5 p.m., June 1 to Labor Day; Sept. to May 31, weekends only, same hours.)** In Virginia, the ruins of a gristmill, house, hotel, and jail mark the site of Matildaville, a busy community in the days when George Washington was supervising work on the first canal to bypass the falls. Extensive picnic and playground facilities make the park ideal for large groups.

CHESAPEAKE & OHIO CANAL

A pleasant trip for footsore sightseers is a ride aboard a mule-drawn barge as it drifts slowly along a restored portion of the historic C. & O. Canal. A National Park Service guide gives an informal commentary on the history and natural features of the canal during the leisurely four-hour trip. Park naturalists also conduct hikes and birdwalks along the towpath, and the canal is used for boating, fishing, and skating in season.

In 1754, young George Washington envisioned a combination of river and canal transportation to service the entire Potomac Valley. After the Revolution, he headed the Potomac Company, which started in 1785 to clear the river and build a series of short canals around its falls. By 1802 rafts were floating furs, lumber, and farm crops from up river to the terminus at Georgetown. To tap the unlimited natural resources of new lands west of the Alleghenies, a far more ambitious scheme was begun in 1828—the construction of a C. & O. Canal to Pittsburgh, 360 miles away. It took more than 20 years to reach Cumberland, Maryland, the halfway point, and that was as far as it ever got.

The restored Georgetown Division parallels the Potomac for 20 miles, a stretch which includes many of the old canal locks and lock houses. The barge is in service from early May to late October. Trips start at Lock 3, just south of 30th and M Sts. in Georgetown.

Departure times are 9 a.m. and 2 p.m. on Sat. and holidays; 2 p.m. only on Sun.; and 6:30 p.m. on Wed. evenings. It is wise to make advance reservations. Organized groups may charter the barge other evenings by phoning Government Services, Inc. at FEderal 7-8080.

Great Falls Tavern (below left), on Maryland side of Potomac,
was built in 1830 as a rest stop on the canal.
Original locks (below right) are still used to lift boats past falls.

EAST POTOMAC PARK

Formerly a swamp, the 328 acres of East Potomac Park are now a pleasant recreation area. To reach it, drive south on 14th St., pass the Jefferson Memorial, and then turn left onto Ohio Drive, the one-way road that circles the park. Japanese cherry trees line the Potomac shore. At the southern tip of the Park, picnic tables are available. In the east center are many recreational facilities, including a golf club with 3 golf courses (1 eighteen-hole, and 2 nine-hole courses), a swimming pool, and a miniature golf course. At the northwest end of the Park are tennis courts. All facilities are public in this beautiful two-mile long recreational mecca.

HAINS POINT, at the park's southern tip, has a new Visitor's Center operated by helpful National Capital Region personnel. Exhibits and illustrated talks give an excellent historic background. Free pamphlets and an itinerary planning service are available. **Open: 9 a.m. to 4:30 p.m., daily, throughout the year.**

WATERGATE, along the Potomac bank behind the Lincoln Memorial, is the site of evening concerts by Army, Navy, Air Force, and Marine Corps bands, June through August.

Riverside concert at Watergate enlivens summer evening.

Boating facilities abound in Washington area. Powerboats (above) are docked in Washington Channel. Cluster of sailboats (right) is berthed at public sailing marina on Daingerfield Island, Virginia.

BOATING

Docking facilities in the Washington area are ample for both powerboats and sailing craft. National Capitol Parks Service operates the Columbia Island Marina, off Mount Vernon Memorial Highway, north of the 14th St. Highway Bridge, where powerboats can be rented or berthed. Phone DIstrict 7-0173. On the same highway, south of National Airport, is the Washington Sailing Marina, which offers moorings and rentals. Call OTis 4-7783 for information. Along Maine Ave., which parallels Washington Channel, are the Capitol and Columbia yacht clubs. Eight other boat clubs are grouped along the lower two and a half miles of the Anacostia River. The Alexandria river front also has public docking and private-club facilities. Still farther south, Chesapeake Bay offers some of the finest boating along the entire Atlantic seaboard.

THEODORE ROOSEVELT ISLAND

This is the kind of memorial that "T. R."—a conservationist and nature enthusiast who expanded the U.S. Forest Service and established many of our national parks—would have picked for himself. The island is situated in the Potomac; it is a mile long and a half mile wide, and has no roads to spoil its wild state. Rich natural habitats of woodland, marsh, and swamp make the island an ideal refuge for a great variety of land and water birds, and small animals.

The National Park Service conducts hour-long nature walks. A ferry runs on weekends from 1 to 4:30 p.m., June through October. It leaves from the foot of Wisconsin Ave. (at K St., N.W.) in Georgetown.

Park ranger directs weekend nature walk about the island.

ROACHES RUN—
A WATERFOWL SANCTUARY

Midway between the Pentagon and National Airport lies a big marshy lagoon that is an ideal haven for migrating ducks and geese, and a seasonal home for herons, egrets, and other shore birds. Mount Vernon Memorial Highway passes the lagoon and a broad traffic turnoff allows plenty of room for parking and observation. (Surprisingly, the birds do not seem to be greatly disturbed by the jet noises from the airport nearby). Although migratory waterfowl are only present in early spring and late fall, shore birds of various kinds live at the sanctuary the year around.

Wild ducks take off from bird sanctuary during fall migrations.

KENILWORTH AQUATIC GARDENS, at Douglas St. and Kenilworth Ave., N.E., lie just off the Anacostia tidal estuary near the District border. Winding paths wander among 14 acres of ponds filled with colorful lotuses and water lilies. Native plants, birds, and animal life abound in the adjacent swamplands. More than 70 types of hardy day-blooming lilies are at their peak by mid-June. In late July and August tropical water lilies and lotuses bloom, some in the daytime, others only after dusk. One lily, the Victoria Cruziana (from the Amazon basin), has leaves up to six feet in diameter. Others range in color from delicate pastels through a deep purple. Umbrella plant and bamboo trees, plus native willow, birch, magnolia, and syca-more, provide shade for both plants and spectators. **Phone LUdlow 2-8302 for tour information.**

THE NATIONAL ARBORETUM covers an area almost a mile square across the Anacostia River from Kenil-worth Gardens (entrance at Maryland and M, N.E.).

Spectacular water lilies (left) in large open ponds at Kenilworth Aquatic Gardens are best seen in the morning, as their blossoms close during hot summer afternoons. Flowering trees and shrubs (right) make springtime ideal season to visit Meridian Hill Park.

Operated by the Department of Agriculture, it contains an extensive collection of trees, shrubs, and plants from all over the world.

ANACOSTIA PARK borders the Anacostia River, includes a recreation center on the east bank (off Anacostia Dr.), a public golf course on the west bank just below the National Arboretum.

MERIDIAN HILL PARK, at 16th and W Sts., N.W. In any other city, this lovely park (directly north of the White House) would be outstanding; amid the tourist wonders of Washington, however, it is often overlooked. Reminiscent of formally designed European parks, it covers 12 landscaped acres. The upper section has a mall, long promenades, and a view of the city. Waterfalls flanked by broad stairways lead to a lower level, whose winding paths are bordered in the spring with dogwood and flowering cherry, rhododendron and azalea. Statues in the park commemorate Dante, James Buchanan, and Joan of Arc.

D.C. STADIUM

22nd & EAST CAPITOL STS., N.E.

Two miles due east of the Capitol is the new home of
the Washington Senators and Redskins (professional
baseball and football teams) and George Washington
University's Colonials. An unusual and architecturally
exciting design allows a large block of seats to be
shifted around the circular stadium, changing the
shape of the playing field for baseball (43,500 seats)
or football (50,000 seats), yet without pillars or visual
obstructions of any kind. The structure covers ten
acres, with another 92 acres of parking space, plus a
helicopter landing pad and docking facilities along
the Anacostia River front.

For schedules and information, phone LIncoln 7-9077.

THE NATIONAL THEATRE, 13th & Pennsylvania, N.W., opened in 1835. It was not the first theater in the capital—strolling players visited Georgetown as early as 1796 and formal theater began in 1804—but it has been the longest lived. In the course of its career the National has burned four times—and been rebuilt each time on the same site. It now draws larger audiences than any legitimate stage outside of New York City, both for out-of-town tryouts and for road company performances of Broadway successes.

ARENA STAGE, 6th & M Sts., S.W., boasts one of the country's most exciting modern theater designs. A theater in the round (where audience sits on all sides of a center stage), it is octagonal in shape and has 752 seats, the farthest ones only eight rows from the performers. It has a full-time professional repertory company that presents Shaw and Shakespeare, light comedy and Eugene O'Neill, and occasionally a new contemporary work. Each play runs for a month. **No performances are given during the summer. Phone 638-6700 for program, times, and prices.**

Lift-away props at Arena Stage simplify scene changes.

The Folger Shakespeare Library, behind the Library of Congress, houses over 250,000 volumes printed between 1475 and 1715, including one of the world's finest collections of Shakespeariana.
While the library facilities are primarily for scholars, the public is welcome to visit an impressive oak-paneled Elizabethan hall that displays historic posters, playbills, costumes, and several First Folios.
Open: 11 a.m. to 4:30 p.m., Mon. through Sat.

VERSATILE WASHINGTON: The capital contains dozens of other interesting places open to the public, some with general appeal, others more specialized: libraries, collections, small private museums, national organizations that maintain their headquarters in the capital. All welcome visitors, but since many are open only half days or on irregular schedules, it's advisable to check their hours by phone.

NATIONAL GUARD ARMORY, 2001 East Capitol St., adjoining the new D.C. Stadium, is used for indoor sporting events, conventions, annual automobile and flower shows, and the Presidential Inaugural Ball.

ZERO MILESTONE, from which all official U.S. mileages are measured, is a small marker standing just south of the White House lawn, on the Ellipse, an oval park often the scene of informal baseball games.

NAVAL OBSERVATORY, 34th & Massachusetts, N.W., has conducted tours at 2 p.m. each weekday. For night tours, when the giant telescope is operating, call the superintendent's office for reservations. (No children under 12 are allowed in the evening.)

132

Union Station, facing a large landscaped area north of the Capitol, was an architectural wonder when completed in 1900.

ROBERT A. TAFT MEMORIAL, a tall carillon, is on the north side of the Capitol, in a triangle bordered by New Jersey, Louisiana, and Constitution Aves.

NATIONAL GEOGRAPHIC SOCIETY, 16th & M, N.W., was founded in 1888. Explorers Hall contains a collection of trophies from Geographic expeditions. **Open: 9:00 a.m. to 4:30 p.m., Mon. through Fri.**

BOOK STORE of the Government Printing Office, North Capitol and G Sts., stocks 30,000 publications, all at nominal prices. (For a catalogue write the Superintendent of Documents, Government Printing Office, Washington 25, D.C. Complete listing: 75 cents. Partial listing: free.)

MARINE BARRACKS, 8th & I Sts., S.E., the oldest post in the Corps, has been in continual use since 1805. It was Marine Corps headquarters until 1901, gave a first hearing to many of John Philip Sousa's famous marches, is now permanent home of the Marine Band. Impressive ceremonial parades are staged each Friday evening from early spring through fall. **Phone LIncoln 3-9400 for times and reservations.**

Shrine of the Immaculate Conception, near Catholic University, is the largest Catholic church in the United States. It boasts a normal seating capacity of some 2,000 persons, and during special services can accommodate as many as 3,000 more. The upper church, completed in 1959, is a combination of Byzantine and Romanesque architectures. A crypt church, consisting of 15 chapels, lies below the main church. The latter was completed in 1932 and is patterned after the Roman catacombs. To the left of the building, a Romanesque campanile, called the Knight's Tower, reaches 329 feet into the air. Guided tours every half hour from Memorial Hall week days, 9 a.m. to 5 p.m.; Sun., noon to 5 p.m. Nearby, at 15th & Quincy, N.E., is a Franciscan monastery. Dating from 1899, it has rose gardens, statues, and chapels. Daily tours: 8 a.m. to 4:30 p.m. for Catacombs; 8 a.m. to 8 p.m. for grounds.

GEORGE WASHINGTON UNIVERSITY, 21st & G, N.W., five blocks due west of the White House, stresses law, government, business, and international affairs; recently started the Institute for Sino-Soviet Studies. **AMERICAN UNIVERSITY** (main campus at Massachusetts and Nebraska Aves., downtown building at 19th and F, N.W.) specializes in law, languages, social and political sciences; schedules government officials and visiting diplomats for graduate-school lectures.

"LIBRARY AND REFERENCE FACILITIES in the District of Columbia" is a valuable brochure for scholars, students, and people with special interests. It lists some 300 collections maintained by government agencies and private organizations, and is available free at the Library of Congress. Sample listings: The Agriculture Department Library of more than 1,000,000 volumes, largest in its field; the U.S. Army map service (nearly 2,000,000 topographic maps).

NATIONAL CAPITAL REGION, National Park Service, has the most varied visitor's program in Washington. Its outdoor schedule runs from April first until late November, will have up to 15 activities scheduled on a busy summer weekend: Hikes, concerts, nature programs, and historical tours for adults and children. During the winter, monthly nature lectures with color slides are presented in the Interior Department auditorium (phone RE 7-1820).

For a yearly program write after March 1 to: Director, National Capital Region, National Park Service, Interior Building, Washington 25, D.C.

National Parks rangers are cheerful, obliging, and full of information. On duty at the major memorials, parks, and historic sites, these knowledgeable men can broaden your understanding of the nation's capital. Don't hesitate to query them on any subject related to the place where they are on duty. They are not just guards, but naturalists, historians, and devoted public servants.

U.S. MARINE CORPS WAR MEMORIAL

The most famous newsphoto of World War II—Joe Rosenthal's picture of the flag raising on Mount Suribachi during the Battle of Iwo Jima—was the model for this memorial sculpted by Felix W. de Welden. Located on a 7½-acre tract, about a quarter mile north of the Arlington Cemetery entrance, the monument re-enacts the historic moment in 32-foot figures, the largest bronze casting ever made. A flag waves day and night from the 60-foot pole. The names and dates of all Marine battles since the Corps was founded in 1775 are inscribed on the black Swedish granite base.

A memorial ceremony is held at the site each Tuesday at 7:30 p.m., June through August.

ARLINGTON NATIONAL CEMETERY

The Potomac has always divided the North and the South, and never more so than when Robert E. Lee stood on the pillared porch of his Virginia home, looked across the river to the city of Washington, and made a fateful decision. Abraham Lincoln had offered him command of the Union armies, but Lee resigned his U.S. Army commission to lead the Confederate forces.

Today the Arlington Memorial Bridge, symbol of a reunited country, spans the river and runs in a straight line from the Lincoln Memorial to the Custis-Lee Mansion (now restored as Arlington House). Built in 1802 by George Washington Parke Custis, a grandson of Martha Washington, it became Lee's home when he married Custis' daughter. After Lee abandoned the 1,100-acre estate, it became a Union army camp. From Arlington House, Julia Ward Howe saw the soldiers' campfires, heard the trumpets, and returned to her hotel to write "The Battle Hymn of the Republic."

Simple marble slabs (left) mark graves of American servicemen buried at Arlington Cemetery, and have since the Civil War, when soldiers of both armies were placed there. Flat-topped headstones indicate the unidentified dead. Right: Netherlands Carillon of 49 bells, each weighing up to six and a half tons, stands half-mile north of cemetery's main gate.

In 1864, the property became a national cemetery for Civil War soldiers. It now shelters veterans of every war the U.S. has fought. Scattered throughout the tree-shaded cemetery is a large number of monuments, statues, and special memorials, the most notable being the Tomb of the Unknowns (pp. 140–141). Another is the memorial to Pierre L'Enfant, who was removed from an obscure grave on a Maryland farm in 1905 and reburied beneath the lawn of Arlington House, facing the city of reality his vision had become.

A memorial area below the Custis-Lee Mansion, which stands on high ground overlooking the Potomac, is the site of the grave of President John F. Kennedy. **Open: Cemetery—7:30 a.m. to 5 p.m., October through March; 7:30 a.m. to 7 p.m., April through September. Arlington House (admission: 25 cents)—9:30 a.m. to 4:30 p.m., October through March; 9:30 a.m. to 6 p.m., April through September.**

Above: Men of the U.S. Army's 3rd Infantry
maintain 24-hour guard at the Tomb of the Unknowns.
Below: Memorial Amphitheater of white
Vermont marble adjoins the tomb.

TOMB OF THE UNKNOWNS

In Arlington Cemetery, three American heroes lie en-shrined on a peaceful Virginia hillside overlooking the capital. Beneath a massive oblong block of Colorado Yule marble is the body of a soldier who died in combat in World War I. The inscription on the stone reads: "Here Rests In Honored Glory An American Soldier Known But To God." At the close of World War I, four unidentified coffins were brought together, one from each of the major military cemeteries in France. In a solemn ceremony a much-decorated sergeant placed a bouquet of white roses on one of the unmarked coffins, which was then brought to Washington to lie in state on the Capitol bier used for Presidents who have died in office. For more than 40 years now, the Unknown Soldier has never been alone—a single guard, rifle on shoulder, paces back and forth before his resting place, night and day, around the clock. Every hour on the hour the guard is changed; time your visit to see it.

In 1958, two more unknown heroes were chosen, one from the far-flung battlefields of World War II, the other from among the fallen in Korea. They lie beneath flat marble slabs on either side of the main stone, marked only by the dates "1941–1945" and "1950–1953." Just to the rear of the three graves is an open oval amphitheater with 5,000 seats. Memorial Day ceremonies and other patriotic gatherings are held here, and a trophy room behind the stage displays decorations and honors that have been conferred on the Unknown Soldiers. Graves and ampitheater are on Roosevelt Drive, one half mile from main gate of Arlington Cemetery.

THE MOUNT VERNON MEMORIAL HIGHWAY, constructed in 1932 to mark the bicentennial of George Washington's birth, is a beautiful scenic parkway linking the capital city with the restored plantation that was the first President's home. Approached via Memorial Bridge (behind the Lincoln Memorial), it parallels the west bank of the Potomac for 15 miles, passing en route many places (map, right) of natural beauty or historic importance. Although impressive at any season, the highway is at its scenic best in the springtime. Flowering crab-apple and pear trees, forsythia and shadbush start the colorful display in early April, followed by redbud and dogwood a fortnight later, and wild azalea's pink blossoms toward the end of the month. May brings roses and mountain laurel, and varicolored day lilies bloom in June and July.

Wildlife abounds in the area, particularly water birds. The highway has frequent parking turnoffs and overlooks from which they may be seen at close range.

Summer brings large numbers of showy white American egrets to the swampy Potomac shores, and our national symbol, the bald eagle, makes its home along the river the year around.

FORT WASHINGTON, Old Fort Rd., off Rt. 210, was the first defense built for the capital. The original fort, finished in 1809, was destroyed in 1814 when the British burned the city. By 1824 it was rebuilt, and at the beginning of the Civil War it was manned once again. Considered an outstanding example of early 19th-century coastal defense, the fort remains in excellent condition. A small museum and information service are at the site. **Open: 10 a.m. to 5 p.m., weekends, May 1 through Labor Day.**

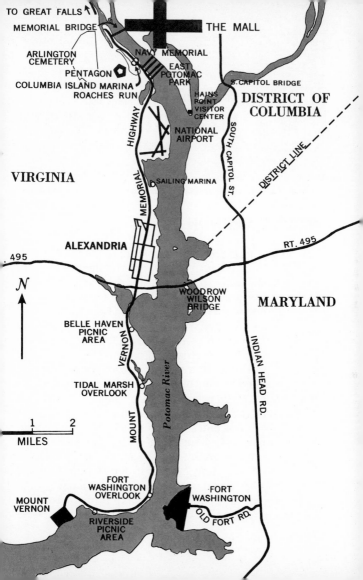

TO GREAT FALLS
MEMORIAL BRIDGE
ARLINGTON CEMETERY
PENTAGON
COLUMBIA ISLAND MARINA
ROACHES RUN

THE MALL

NAVY MEMORIAL
EAST POTOMAC PARK
S. CAPITOL BRIDGE

HAINS POINT VISITOR CENTER

DISTRICT OF COLUMBIA

DISTRICT LINE

VIRGINIA

NATIONAL AIRPORT

MEMORIAL HIGHWAY

SOUTH CAPITOL ST.

SAILING MARINA

ALEXANDRIA

RT. 495

495

N

WOODROW WILSON BRIDGE

MARYLAND

BELLE HAVEN PICNIC AREA

MOUNT VERNON

TIDAL MARSH OVERLOOK

Potomac River

INDIAN HEAD RD.

1 2
MILES

FORT WASHINGTON OVERLOOK

FORT WASHINGTON

MOUNT VERNON

RIVERSIDE PICNIC AREA

OLD FORT RD.

Manor-house west facade faces bowling green, other side overlooks Potomac.

MOUNT VERNON

"No estate in United America is more pleasantly situated than this. It lies in a high, dry and healthy country 300 miles by water from the sea . . . on one of the finest rivers in the world . . . in a latitude between the extremes of heat and cold." This description of his beloved home, written more than 150 years ago by George Washington, remains true today. The lovely plantation on the Potomac has been carefully restored to its appearance during Washington's later years, is easily reached by car, bus, or boat. To avoid crowds in the spring or summer, it is best to arrive early. The beautifully landscaped Mount Vernon Memorial Highway leads to the entrance, 15 miles from the capital. Buses leave every hour from a terminal at Pennsylvania Ave. and 12th St., and an excursion boat leaves Main and N St., S.W., 10 a.m. and 2 p.m., June 1 through Labor Day. Lunch is available on the grounds. **Open: 9 a.m. to 5 p.m., daily, March through September; 9 a.m. to 4 p.m., the rest of the year.**

144

Washington's great grandfather John acquired the estate in 1674, and George eventually became the owner by inheriting 2,700 acres from an older half brother in 1754. He gradually built the property up to 8,000 acres, which were divided into five separate farms. Each was a self-supporting unit—four for large-scale planting and the fifth as a manor house, with outbuildings, gardens, fields, and woods just as they are seen now. Although Washington was away from Mount Vernon for long periods (eight years during the Revolution, another eight as President), its welfare was close to his heart. He kept in touch with its activities and guided its improvements during his absence through correspondence with his manager. On the working farms, 125 field hands grew corn, wheat, and flax as cash crops under a five-year crop-rotation plan. The wheat was ground in a gristmill and brought top prices on the market. Resident bricklayers, blacksmiths, carpenters, bakers, and brewers made the big plantation virtually independent of the outside world.

Formal flower garden, surrounded by boxwood hedges, stands to the left of the bowling green that stretches before manor house. Fruit trees, annuals, perennials common to Virginia gardens in the late 18th century still bloom there. The small circular building in the distance was once a schoolhouse.

Authentic regional furnishings of the period supplement many known original pieces in the Mount Vernon mansion. Like most well-to-do country gentlemen of the time, Washington had the finest available furniture in his home, much of it made abroad to special order. He personally planned the manor house, acting as his own architect. The building appears to be made of cut stone, but this was simulated by beveling the wood siding and sprinkling sand into the fresh white paint. A columned piazza running the full length of the east front provides a magnificent view of the Potomac and is the building's outstanding feature. After many years away from home, the commander in chief of the Continental armies had earnestly hoped to retire to peace and quiet, but, as he said in a letter of 1787, ". . . in truth it (Mount Vernon) may be compared to a well restored tavern, as scarcely any strangers who are going from north to south, or from south to north, do not spend a day or two at it." Always a modest individual, Washington found his fame embarrassing, but as a courteous Virginia gentleman, he put up with it.

Among Washington's valued belongings displayed in the mansion are (left to right): the key to the Bastille (a gift from Lafayette in 1790), a mirrored plateau and classical figurine used as centerpiece, and a grandfather clock. Right: Over the mantel in west parlor is carved pediment. Center panel, under Washington family coat of arms, is graced by English landscape.

Today's visitor to Mount Vernon finds the entire estate restored with careful attention to the smallest details—even the facing property across the Potomac has been acquired to preserve the view! The 500 acres of grounds were the original manor-house farm and contain all the outbuildings—kitchen, laundry, icehouse, smokehouse, servants' quarters, coach house, stables —that existed at the time of Washington's death.

Both floors of the mansion itself are open to the public. A spacious banquet hall begins the tour, followed by a comfortable parlor and the music room, where George's step-granddaughter Nellie Custis played a harpsichord. A large central hall allowed summer breezes through the width of the house, and the library was Washington's personal retreat. The family dining room, pantry, and a bedroom complete the lower floor. Upstairs, six bedrooms (plus three more in the attic) were none too many for an almost continuous stream of visitors. The President's bedroom contains his over-sized bed (he was over six feet), the trunk he used during the Revolution, and other furnishings.

ALEXANDRIA

This was the county seat for George Washington's part of tidewater Virginia. Here he came to Christ Church, Gadsby's Tavern, social affairs, and Masonic meetings. Nine miles from Mount Vernon, it took about two hours to reach by coach, today is only a few minutes by car. Walk around its historic streets, where many of the old red-brick houses date from pre-Revolutionary times. During the spring a house-and-garden tour provides a look behind some of the more elaborate colonial doorways; check the Alexandria Chamber of Commerce for dates. The George Washington Masonic National Memorial, south of the city, houses murals and dioramas of his life (he was first Master of the Alexandria lodge), and from the front steps there is a sweeping six-mile view up the Potomac to the capital the modest Washington always called "Federal City."

Masonic Memorial.   **Christ Church (1767–73).**

Beautiful Skyline Drive is only two hours from capital.

SHENANDOAH NATIONAL PARK and its 105-mile Skyline Drive stretches north-south along the crest of the Blue Ridge Mountains of western Virginia. Some 300 square miles of wilderness area, first explored by John Lederer in 1669, are today crisscrossed with hiking trails so that visitors to the park may wander freely along its peaks. Campgrounds, trailer sites, and inns provide overnight accommodations, and picnic benches are regularly spaced along the road. For the auto tourist, 75 panoramic overlooks afford magnificent vistas of the Shenandoah countryside. Elevations within the park reach 4,049 feet at the summit of Hawksbill, and 4,010 feet atop Stony Man.

MANASSAS NATIONAL BATTLEFIELD PARK marks the site of the First and Second Battles of Bull Run (1861, 1862), both of which were Confederate victories. Battle positions are indicated by Park Service plaques: the old stone bridge that was a key point of action still stands, as does the stone house that served as a hospital. Mementos may be seen at visitor's center. The park is 26 miles west of Washington on Rts. 29 and 211. **Open: 9 a.m. to 5 p.m. daily.**

Bancroft Hall is world's largest dormitory.
It houses the entire brigade of midshipmen—two
men to a room—at U.S. Naval Academy.

ANNAPOLIS, Maryland, 33 miles east of Washington on Rt. 50, is a beautiful old city containing some of the finest Georgian architecture in the U.S. Its tall brick State House was built in 1772, has since been in continuous use as Maryland's capitol. Many of the magnificent old homes of Annapolis have belonged to the same families for more than 200 years.

U.S. NAVAL ACADEMY, founded in 1845, welcomes visitors to the Annapolis area daily from 9 a.m. to 7 p.m. See the tomb of John Paul Jones in the chapel, the naval museum, and Bancroft Hall, which houses the entire 4,000-man brigade. An example of a midshipman's room is exhibited. Murals of naval battles may be seen in the rotunda. **Dress parades are scheduled Wednesdays at 3:30 p.m. in spring and fall.**

TOURIST TIPS

Washington is a friendly town with much of the courtesy of the Old South. Don't hesitate to ask questions. Guards at the major memorials and museums are proud of their particular attraction and have voluminous and accurate information about it.

Each spring thousands of students see Washington on economical all-expense tours. The most popular package provides three days and two nights in town, accommodations at better hotels or luxury motels, meals in good restaurants and cafeterias. Sightseeing includes major points in the city, Mount Vernon and Arlington, a half-day free time for personal preferences.

In summer the city is crowded with family groups, and advance reservations are essential to avoid ending up in a motel 30 miles away. Washington can be extremely hot and humid, although most buildings are air-conditioned. Wear comfortable clothes and walking shoes, but remember this is a city, not a beach resort. Dress with respect for the places you will visit.

Fall is the time for hiking along the C. & O. Canal, a stroll through Georgetown or along Embassy Row, and a visit to the zoo. When the leaves turn color the city's multitude of parks are at their best.

Crisp, sunny winter days are fine for brisk walks to the Smithsonian and uncrowded art galleries, time to see Congress or the Supreme Court in action, visit your senator or representative.

Washington's business district (the area east of the White House, running about six blocks in each direction) contains large department stores, first-run movie houses, some of the city's best restaurants and hotels.

Good weather brings baseball to field near Washington Monument.

Your hotel or motel will gladly help organize your trip, confirm visiting hours, suggest eating places. A guided tour shows the most in the least time, can be arranged for at your hotel, will hit the high spots and get you oriented. Four-hour bus tours run about $5.50 (half fare for children under 12), include the interiors of several key buildings and a ride past two dozen others, with a continuous lecture. An all-day trip for $14 also covers Arlington, Alexandria, and Mount Vernon.

The key to seeing Washington lies in a careful study of visiting hours. Mark the places open beyond 6 p.m. with an N; those with daylight hours mark with a D. Put your car in a ramp garage downtown. Leave it there until after 6:30 p.m. Plan to see the D places on foot, by bus, or by taxi. Drive to the N places in the evening when traffic is lighter.

THREE TOURS

ONE DAY in Washington calls for tight scheduling and an early start. Arrive at the Washington Monument shortly before it opens at 8 a.m. (get there earlier during crowded Easter week) for a view from the top. Back on the ground with directions in mind, walk northward to the White House in time for the special tour. (This is the only one for which reservations can be made. Write your congressman well in advance of your trip.)

After a brief peek at Lafayette Park, opposite the White House, take a cab or bus along Pennsylvania Ave. to the Capitol. Here the standard 45-minute tour is all you'll have time for. Allow half an hour each in the Library of Congress and the Supreme Court building. Take the tours at both places if there is no waiting, otherwise look around on your own.

Try to limit yourself to an hour at the National Gallery. Proceed northwest across Constitution Ave. to the National Archives (20 minutes), diagonally back again to the Mall, the Natural History Building, and the new Museum of History and Technology next door. After an hour in each it will be almost 5 o'clock and you'll once again be near the Washington Monument. Take an hour's rest, have a leisurely dinner, then onward to the Jefferson Memorial. Wind up a busy day at the Lincoln Memorial, seen at its magnificent best after dark.

THREE DAYS permit a much more leisurely pace. Start out the same way as on the one-day tour, avoiding waiting on lines with early visits to the Washington Monument and White House. Proceed to Capitol Hill and start with the official tour, but then take your time and browse around the massive old building on your own.

Ask questions! Typical behind-the-scenes information: Lincoln bust in Capitol Rotunda was preliminary study for Gutzon Borglum's huge sculptures on Mount Rushmore.

Visit your congressman at the House Office Building, then come back for lunch at the Senate dining room. After a good look through the Supreme Court and the Library of Congress, take a walk around the Capitol grounds, stopping off at the Botanic Gardens. Stroll down the Mall, turning north at 7th St. to the National Archives, then next door to the Department of Justice and the F.B.I. tour. In the early evening visit the Lincoln and Jefferson Memorials and Ford's Theatre.

Start the SECOND DAY with a driving and walking trip around historic Georgetown and along Embassy Row. Stop at the Islamic Center, then go farther out Massachusetts Ave. to the Washington Cathedral. After lunch, drive (or bus) to Mount Vernon, stopping on the way back at Christ Church in Alexandria, the Tomb of the Unknown Soldier in Arlington National Cemetery, and the Marine Memorial nearby. In the evening take a stroll through the downtown business district.

On the THIRD DAY begin with the National Gallery, followed by the Museum of History and Technology and the Natural History Building. In the afternoon cross the Mall to the Air Museum and the Freer Gallery; also, see currency being made at the Bureau of Engraving & Printing. Or visit the zoo and Rock Creek Park. At night, try one of the theaters or arenas.

A WEEK in Washington not only permits the visitor to see much more, but gives him a chance to arrange his trip in a logical way. As on the shorter trips, start by orienting yourself from the top of the Washington Monument. Spend a full day around Capitol Hill (or more if Congress is in session) if politics and the science of government intrigue you. In addition to the Capitol, Supreme Court, and Library of Congress, visit the Folger Shakespeare Library. Give your second day to the White House, the major memorials, any executive departments that interest you, Lafayette Park, and the downtown shopping district. Allow the third day for Mount Vernon, Alexandria, and Arlington (the National Cemetery, Tomb of the Unknown Soldier, Marine Memorial). Devote the fourth day entirely to museums—the many branches of the Smithsonian and any of the others that excite your interest. (This could easily stretch to two days.) Combine Georgetown, Embassy Row, and the Washington Cathedral into one trip; it can be rushed through in a half day, but will be enjoyed far more by taking longer. Divide a full day outdoors among the Great Falls of the Potomac, the C. & O. Canal, and Rock Creek Park. Don't miss the zoo. Save the last day for anything you've missed.

SPECIAL INTEREST TOURS: The Washington visitor with a professional or hobby interest in a particular field can set up his own tours. Here are some hints.

ARCHITECTURE: Aside from major memorials and classic government buildings, don't miss Georgetown, Lafayette Square, Mt. Vernon, and Alexandria for a feeling of the 18th century. Three churches are exceptional: Washington Cathedral, Shrine of the Immaculate Conception, and the Islamic Center. For modern design see the D.C. Stadium, Arena Stage and adjacent Town Center redevelopment at 4th & K, S.W.

HISTORY: Aside from the obvious landmarks, visit the Smithsonian's new Museum of History and Technology, the Corcoran's collection of early American paintings, the Truxton-Decatur Museum, and Church of the Presidents. Outside of town, try Fort Washington, Manassas battlefield, the C. & O. Canal museum at Great Falls—as well as Mt. Vernon and Alexandria. Check with National Capital Region, National Park Service, for tours, lectures.

NATURE: First check the Nature Center at Rock Creek Park for a schedule of special outdoor programs. Nature hikes can be made along the towpath of the C. & O. Canal and on Theodore Roosevelt Island. Bird watching is fine at Roaches Run. The National Arboretum and Kenilworth Aquatic Gardens are well worth the trip.

ART: Major galleries are listed on contents page; all are worth while. Don't overlook the Phillips Gallery, 21st & Q, along Embassy Row, and the new Washington Gallery of Modern Art, 1502 21st St. N.W.

Spectacular fireworks display on grounds of Washington Monument is a traditional July 4th event best seen from Tidal Basin area.

BIBLIOGRAPHY

Ogg & Ray, ESSENTIALS OF AMERICAN GOVERNMENT, Appleton-Century-Crofts, revised 1959. The classic college text, complete and extremely detailed.

Binkley, W. E. & Moos, M. C., A GRAMMAR OF AMERICAN POLITICS, Alfred A. Knopf, revised 1958. Politicians and political parties, how they operate.

Laski, Harold, THE AMERICAN PRESIDENCY, Grosset & Dunlap, 1940. Old but still excellent short study of the executive branch.

White, T. H., THE MAKING OF THE PRESIDENT 1960, Atheneum Publishers, 1961, and Pocket Books Cardinal edition, 1962. Superb journalistic coverage of 1960 campaigns.

Matthews, Donald R., U.S. SENATORS AND THEIR WORLD, University of North Carolina Press, 1960.

Galloway, Geo. B., A HISTORY OF THE HOUSE OF REPRESENTATIVES, Thos. Y. Crowell Co., 1961.

Beard, Charles A., THE SUPREME COURT AND THE CONSTITUTION, Prentice-Hall, 1912, revised 1962. Classic study with a new introduction.

Schlesinger, Arthur M. Jr., THE AGE OF JACKSON, Little, Brown & Co., 1945. (Period: 1829–1840)

Leech, Margaret, REVEILLE IN WASHINGTON, Harper & Bros., 1941. (Period: 1860–1863)

Carpenter, Frank G., CARP'S WASHINGTON, McGraw-Hill Book Co., 1960. (Period: 1880–1900)

Drury, Allen, ADVISE AND CONSENT, Doubleday & Co. 1959, Pocket Books Cardinal edition, 1961. Pulitzer Prize novel with Capitol Hill background.

THE WHITE HOUSE, an historic guide, 1962. 132 pages, beautifully reproduced drawings and photographs in color. Available on White House tour. Price: $1.

FREE PAMPHLETS on all major memorials and historic locations under National Capital Region, National Park Service jurisdiction are available on sites.

INDEX

158

CDEFGH